21st CENTURY
TECHNOLOGIES

PROMISES AND PERILS
OF A DYNAMIC FUTURE

ORGANISATION FOR ECONOMIC CO-OPERATION AND DEVELOPMENT

ORGANISATION FOR ECONOMIC CO-OPERATION AND DEVELOPMENT

Pursuant to Article 1 of the Convention signed in Paris on 14th December 1960, and which came into force on 30th September 1961, the Organisation for Economic Co-operation and Development (OECD) shall promote policies designed:

- to achieve the highest sustainable economic growth and employment and a rising standard of living in Member countries, while maintaining financial stability, and thus to contribute to the development of the world economy;
- to contribute to sound economic expansion in Member as well as non-member countries in the process of economic development; and
- to contribute to the expansion of world trade on a multilateral, non-discriminatory basis in accordance with international obligations.

The original Member countries of the OECD are Austria, Belgium, Canada, Denmark, France, Germany, Greece, Iceland, Ireland, Italy, Luxembourg, the Netherlands, Norway, Portugal, Spain, Sweden, Switzerland, Turkey, the United Kingdom and the United States. The following countries became Members subsequently through accession at the dates indicated hereafter: Japan (28th April 1964), Finland (28th January 1969), Australia (7th June 1971), New Zealand (29th May 1973), Mexico (18th May 1994), the Czech Republic (21st December 1995), Hungary (7th May 1996), Poland (22nd November 1996) and Korea (12th December 1996). The Commission of the European Communities takes part in the work of the OECD (Article 13 of the OECD Convention).

Publié en français sous le titre :

LES TECHNOLOGIES DU XXIᵉ SIÈCLE :
PROMESSES ET PÉRILS D'UN FUTUR DYNAMIQUE

FOREWORD

As part of the preparations for EXPO 2000 – the World Exposition in Hannover, Germany – the OECD Forum for the Future is organising a series of four conferences to take place beforehand around the theme of "People, Nature and Technology: Sustainable Societies in the 21st Century". The series will consider four key areas of human activity: technology, economy, society and government. The conferences will explore possible evolutions of key variables and analyse different development paths in order to expose some of the main policy implications and options. Each conference will provide analysis of underlying trends and policy directions. However, the overall aim of the series is to build a comprehensive foundation for assessing the critical choices likely to face citizens and decision-makers in the next century.

The entire series is benefiting from special sponsorship by EXPO 2000 and four German banks – Bankgesellschaft Berlin, DG BANK Deutsche Genossenschaftsbank, NORD/LB Norddeutsche Landesbank, and Westdeutsche Landesbank Girozentrale (WestLB). Additional financial support is provided by numerous Asian, European and North American partners of the OECD Forum for the Future.

The first of these conferences, hosted by the Westdeutsche Landesbank (WestLB), was held at Schloss Krickenbeck near Düsseldorf, Germany 7-8 December 1997. The theme was "21st Century Technologies: Balancing Economic, Social and Environmental Goals".

Shaping the future in order to realise economic and social goals is one of the fundamental challenges of human society. Technology has proved key in meeting this challenge, and its role appears set to remain at least as important in the future. However, there are many uncertainties with regard to the transformation of technological potential into positive economic and social outcomes. Indeed, for many people displaced at work or bewildered by new, unfamiliar products, it seems as if technological progress is more of a curse than a blessing. This first conference examined both the positive and the negative sides, the opportunities and the risks, that may arise as technology develops over the next twenty-five years. In so doing, it explored the two-way relationship between technology on the one hand and economy and society on the other.

The conference was organised into three sessions. The first assessed general trends in pervasive technologies, particularly information and biological technologies, with the aim of identifying areas of technically feasible future applications. The second session explored how different economic, social and political frameworks might lead to differences in the extent to which technological opportunities are realised and risks reduced. In the concluding session, the focus was on the policy directions most likely to enhance the contribution of technology to the realisation of sustainable economic, social and environmental goals.

This publication brings together the papers presented at the meeting as well as an introductory contribution and summary of the main points of the discussions prepared by the Secretariat. The book is published on the responsibility of the Secretary-General of the OECD.

TABLE OF CONTENTS

THE PROMISES AND PERILS
OF 21st CENTURY TECHNOLOGY:
AN OVERVIEW OF THE ISSUES

by

Riel Miller, Wolfgang Michalski and Barrie Stevens
OECD Secretariat, Advisory Unit to the Secretary-General

Over the past century there have been many profound technological, economic and social transformations. In OECD countries the full development and diffusion of innovations such as electricity, telephones and automobiles have accompanied the emergence of mass production, mass consumption and mass government. There are many who, facing the next century, wonder if it will be possible and/or desirable to continue along the path of such prodigious change. Some worry about the capacity, both technological and social, to continue advancing and inventing new tools, new products and new ways of organising everyday work and home life. Others worry that the ongoing transition costs may be too high, or that the risks to cherished traditions or the threats to environmental sustainability will, singly or together, be too great to bear. Preservation versus dynamism, incrementalism versus radicalism, these are the polar extremes that, unsurprisingly, haunt many end-of-the-century, future-of-the-millennium debates.

The OECD Forum for the Future Conference on 21st Century Technologies was no exception; all of these perspectives were analysed and discussed. However, perhaps the most striking thing about the conference was the widely held view that the prospects for prosperity – economic, social and environmental – over the next twenty-five years will probably hinge on actively encouraging changes equal to, if not greater than, those already experienced in the twentieth century. In particular, realising the full potential of tomorrow's technologies to contribute to human well-being was seen as depending heavily on the capacity to embrace dynamic change. With only a few reservations, the analysis affirmed the benefits of pursuing socio-technical dynamism rather than preservationism. The analysis also underscored the urgency of pushing beyond incremental and *ad hoc* reactive approaches in order to develop and implement more transformative and integrated economic, social and technological courses of action.

This introductory chapter is divided into three sections. The first focuses on the prospects for twenty-first century technologies – largely ignoring economic or social factors – given the current state of play in today's research and development labs. The second considers the crucial economic and social forces – at micro, macro and global levels – that are likely to play key roles in determining both the path of technological development and its diffusion. Lastly, the chapter offers an assessment of policy initiatives that might foster the most beneficial patterns of technological development and distribution.

I. ENVISIONING TECHNOLOGY'S POTENTIAL: OPPORTUNITIES AND RISKS

Imagining possible applications of technology two or three decades from now calls for a better understanding of the ways in which performance trends interact with societies' readiness to embrace economic, social and technical change. In venturing a vision of technological possibilities rather than simply projecting linear or exponential changes in performance, it is crucial to think not only of how technical improvements lead to the substitution of a new generation of tools for existing ones, but also of how entirely new uses, and indeed new needs, might emerge.

Significant progress is likely across a broad spectrum of technologies, discussed in Joseph Coates' contribution to this volume: computing, genetics, brain technology, new materials (in particular miniaturisation and smart composites), energy, transportation and environmental tools and systems. The technical foundation (as distinct from the economic and social) for this continuing wave of innovation will emerge, in large part, from powerful developments in the fields of digital and genetic information. The exploration and manipulation of these two building blocks – one of calculation, the other of nature – are likely to unlock vast treasures for both tool-builders and -users. Indeed, there seems to be a strong virtuous circle between better information and higher performance tools, as each insight provided by digital computation or genetic mapping (still at an early stage) helps to drive forward new ideas about how to design and use technology.

This complementarity is particularly powerful in the digital realm. Improvements in the quantity and quality of the information transformed into strings of zeros and ones are allowing rapid advances to be made in many other domains of science and engineering.

Advances in the performance and use of digital information

Performance

One way of tracking technological change over time (and into the future) is to consider measurements of speed, size or cost. From this perspective, progress is easy to calibrate. Twenty-five years ago a megabyte of semiconductor memory cost around $550 000; today it costs around $4. Microprocessors in 1997 were 100 000 times faster than the 1950 originals. Should these trends continue – and there are many experts who think they will – by 2020 one desktop computer will be as powerful as all of the computers currently in Silicon Valley.

Faster, cheaper, smaller are more than slogans for the highly competitive information technology sector, as will become clear in the chapter by Hervé Gallaire. In the development pipeline are a number of improvements that might even accelerate the already rapid pace of cost/performance improvement. For example, there is a good chance that mixed optical/silicon computers will come into widespread use. This will allow laser beams to transmit data within a computer chip, thereby overcoming some of the bottlenecks – such as excessive heat – that arise from miniaturisation of circuits on semiconductors. Developments in low-temperature superconducting and new refrigeration methods will also allow improvements in processing power. Quantum mechanical computing appears to be on the horizon, promising potentially large gains in computation speeds. All told, the prospects for the key component of computing technology – the microprocessor – look very promising.

Network technology as well will continue to move forward along a path that delivers both greater diversity and much higher bandwidth. Heavy-duty transmission systems will lean on ever-faster fibre optical systems, while mobile communications coverage will rain down from a variety of low- and high-orbit satellites. A larger part of the available frequency spectrum will be better used by digital broadcasts and compression methods that allow high-density data flows to reach a wide variety of locations and devices. Home installation of a personal network (PN) will become affordable. For users, communication services may not quite reach zero cost, but they will be close to it by the third decade of the next century.

Considerable progress will likely be made in improving the human-computer interface, largely because voice and gesture recognition will have been perfected. Instantaneous real-time translation may also be quite close to fully functional by 2025. All audio, video and text-based data sources will be in digital form and amenable to universal searches. Most current computer-related security, privacy and inter-operability questions will have been resolved, allowing for the same degree of confidence (sometimes more, *via* instant verification) that currently obtains when it comes to face-to-face transactions and communication.

Semiconductor-based sensors, some at the molecular or atomic level and integrated with DNA, will be able inexpensively to collect vast quantities of highly precise environmental and biological information, and begin to open up new frontiers for direct human-machine interconnection.

One potential brake on performance improvements in the field of IT could be software. Many analysts see only modest advances in the area of "artificial intelligence" over the next two decades. The quest for software that is fully capable of undertaking autonomous thought and able to respond with inference and creativity to human conversation will probably continue well into the middle of the next century. However, intelligent agents capable of accumulating data about an individual's tastes and behavioural patterns are likely to emerge over this period. Considerable progress is also expected in the development of VRML (Virtual Reality markup language), a three-dimensional version of the text-based HTML (hypertext markup language) that currently dominates Web pages on the Internet.

Uses

Twenty-five years from now, after more than five decades of development, the microprocessor, information technologies in general, and networks will probably have penetrated every aspect of human activity. Many parts of the world will be wired, responsive and interactive. Beyond simply accelerating the pace of change or reducing the cost of many current activities, the use of these high-performance digital tools opens up the possibility of profound transformations.

There is a good chance that the advanced power of computing will be used to help people stay in or create new kinds of communities, both virtual and real. In some parts of the world this could mean a return to villages and less urban settings. In other regions, perhaps where there is better infrastructure or other attractions, people will stick to their "silicon alley". In either case, the use of computing power will allow us to make choices about where and how we live and work that were not possible before. The trade-offs imposed by distance will change in the networked world of 2025. Physical isolation no longer needs to impose as great an economic or social penalty.

The use of computing power will greatly enhance possibilities in production, transportation, energy, commerce, education and health. For instance, industrial robots will most likely become ubiquitous as the better software and hardware allow them to take on onerous, dangerous, high-precision or miniaturised tasks in many sectors of the economy. They will also be employed in deep sea and outer space operations. Computers will probably influence the environmental costs of transportation by both improving vehicle design/engineering (hybrid cars, hydrogen fuel-cell engines, etc.) and traffic management. In the field of energy production and conservation, whole new horizons will open up as computers and networks reduce the costs and risks of co-generation and allow the proliferation of local management of energy production and use. Powerful computers will make it easier to design products that are more environmentally sustainable because the production process is less wasteful and the end-product can be recycled, reused or remanufactured.

At a broader level, computer-enabled development of electronic commerce is likely to profoundly modify current ways of doing business. Anyone with a computer and Internet access will be in a position to become a merchant and reach out to customers across the globe, and any consumer will be able to shop the world for goods and services. As a result, new products and services and new markets should emerge, many a traditional role of intermediary could disappear, and more direct relations will probably be forged between businesses and consumers. Indeed, the process of inventing and selling products could be turned on its head, as consumers generate the custom specifications they desire and then seek out competent producers and even other buyers.

As for the inquiry and collaboration that are indispensable for learning and basic scientific research, the power of tomorrow's Information Technologies will open up new vistas by radically improving the capacity to communicate and simulate. Virtual Reality's capacity to mimic historical and physical situations might mean that learning by "doing", joint experimental research and moving at one's own pace are all within every "wired" person's grasp. Once liberated from some of the cost, time and space constraints of traditional education, it might even be possible to get beyond the socialisation methods of industrial era schooling to create a system that encourages individual creativity.

In order to avoid drowning in an ocean of information, people will probably use "knowbots" (knowledge robots) to navigate effectively. Virtual robots with fairly narrowly defined tasks, a type of expert software, will have reached the point of being able to track and respond to many human needs, from the banal capacity of a networked toaster to identify users and recall their preferences to the more advanced functionality of e-mail screening, comparison shopping and assembling/tracking a person's customised learning "adventures." And in the field of healthcare, self-contained portable sensing and diagnostic equipment linked up to remote expert systems could bring about significant improvements in patient mobility and hospital resource efficiency.

Advances in the performance and use of genetic information

Performance

The identification of genetic information and applications of genetic engineering are already making their mark in many of areas of human activity. While they are unlikely to have quite the same pervasive impact as Information

Technology on the organisational aspects of economy and society, they will none-theless profoundly affect many facets of everyday life. Those that stand out most from today's perspective are human health, food production (livestock, plants) and food processing, and activities at the crossroads between genetics and other technologies.

Work is already well under way on the human genome, a subject taken up in the chapter by Werner Arber and Mathis Brauchbar. By 2005, after fifteen years of intense activity, scientists should know the full DNA sequence of a typical man or woman. Although at present only a very small percentage of this information has been mapped, the pace of discovery is expected to accelerate dramatically. As the average cost of sequencing each of the millions of DNA base pairs rapidly diminishes – from $5 in 1990 to less than fifty cents by the beginning of the next century – the number of DNA base pairs sequenced each year is rising exponen-tially: from around 40 million in 1990 to over 400 million in 1997. In parallel, the next twenty-five years could see major breakthroughs in disentangling the com-plexity of the human body's biochemical pathways along which genetic informa-tion is transferred, and in understanding how certain genes interact with environ-mental influences to exert different effects on different people.

What the next twenty-five years are likely to witness is the identification and mapping of the genomes of thousands of prototypical creatures – mammals, fish, insects, micro-organisms and plants. Large-scale initiatives are currently close to implementation. In the United States, for example, the National Science Founda-tion has launched a major $40 million Plant Genome Initiative, and the Depart-ment of Agriculture is working towards a $200 million National Food Genome Strategy. As the biochemical pathways of gene transfer are worked out for animal and plant life forms, vast possibilities could open up for the refined management, control and manipulation of their health, propagation or elimination. Routine genetic programmes could emerge for enhancing animals and plants, leading to faster breeding cycles, accelerated plant evolution, and the development of increasing numbers of patentable varieties. Twenty years from now, virtually every widely distributed seed could have been influenced in one way or another (*i.e.* through cross-fertilization or genetic manipulation) by genetic engineering.

But perhaps the most dramatic breakthroughs in the not-too-distant future will be achieved through combinations of various scientific disciplines. For exam-ple, work cutting across biochemistry, physics, molecular biology, neurosciences, biotechnology, nanotechnology and microelectronics looks set to make significant advances in the field of bioelectronics (*e.g.* the development of biosensors) and neuroinformatics (linking microprocessing with the human nervous system). With the expected trend toward greater diversification of R&D spending on genetics into chemicals, materials, energy technologies, etc., major advances in other cross-disciplinary fields could take on significant proportions – *e.g.* the creation of synthesised gene-derived enzyme catalysts, non-existent in nature, for use in chemical engineering; biological processes to fabricate molecular structures and more complex materials; bioengineered plants to produce pharmaceuticals and raw materials for plastics.

Uses

Biotechnology applications are likely to pervade most areas of activity in the next quarter-century. Already well entrenched and expanding in human health, animal husbandry, plant agriculture and food processing, they could find their way increasingly into environmental management, manufacturing processes, new materials and computers.

It is in human health that most people expect the greatest progress over the next decades. With the mapping of the human genome and the identification of biochemical transmission routes and of genetic predispositions, genetic testing could become routine. Therapies for single-gene and even some multiple-gene disorders could be widespread by 2025, as could gene replacement therapy. The prescription of gene-based pharmaceuticals might by then be commonplace – for example, those using antisense DNA to block the body's process of transmitting genetic instructions to trigger a disease process. Concretely, disorders transmitted by a single gene, such as Huntington's Chorea and cystic fibrosis as well as certain types of Alzheimer's disease, arthritis and cancer, could by 2025 be both treatable and possibly reversible. Thanks to advances in interdisciplinary research, life expectancy and physical mobility could be further enhanced: with the increasingly standard application of biosensors in diagnosis; and, in surgery, the use of sensor implants, neuronal prostheses (*e.g.* for simulating hearing or restoring the functions of paralysed limbs) and even organ cloning.

The impact on the delivery of healthcare promises to be fundamental. It is not simply a matter of treatments becoming much more individualised. The quantum leap in genetic knowledge, information, diagnosis, prevention and therapy, combined with continuing progress in other technologies (notably IT) would mean – at least in the more advanced societies – more personal control over health and more possibilities for self-treatment, and thus more lifestyle choices. As a result, healthcare delivery could become much more decentralised. Indeed, the practice of medicine, increasingly encroached upon by research, self-diagnosis and self-treatment, may gradually be obliged to take a back seat.

With numerous prototypical animals, plants, insects and micro-organisms mapped and their gene delivery systems worked out, major avenues would open up for applications in food and agriculture. Genetically modified plants are increasingly common – in 1997 American farmers planted some 10 million hectares with genetically engineered seeds, and across the world some two dozen varieties of genetically modified plants are in use. It is not difficult to conceive of routine production of transgenic customised livestock, fruit and vegetables, forming the basis for widespread consumption of "designer" food and new varieties and products. Transgenic sheep, pigs and cows may be kept as living factories to produce proteins and other much sought-after compounds, for example in their milk, or may be modified to resist particularly harsh climates. Aquaculture would have at its disposal genetic engineering techniques to refine the different tastes and textures of seafood. Crop plants and forest stocks across the world could be modified for inbuilt pest resistance, insecticidal or chemical properties, better storage, and greater adaptation to specific environmental conditions.

The outcome would be the prospect of significantly improved diets and greatly expanded food choices for consumers. For producers, it would mean nothing less than a radical transformation of farming practices and structures. Farmers will face a wide range of options as to new varieties, new products, and the degree of animal or crop specialisation they would need to pursue. New types of producer could enter the arena (*e.g.* pharmaceutical companies rearing transgenic animals for specific substances), and relations between producers, processors, retailers and consumers would likely be transformed by the emergence of highly specified, highly customised ordering systems.

Risks associated with advances in new technologies

Still, with all this scientific promise, there are myriad risks that could be provoked or exacerbated by tomorrow's plausible technological innovations. As has been the case ever since technologies were employed not only for survival but also for conflict, these tools often have a double edge. Technological advances *per se* provide no foregone conclusions about how they will be used. Indeed, looked at purely from the perspective of technical feasibility – without taking into account the economic and social safeguards that are likely to be prerequisites for the rapid emergence of tomorrow's technological breakthroughs – three broad dangers can be identified.

First, tomorrow's technologies contain destructive potential that will be both powerful and difficult to control. They could pose threats to the natural and human environment. Either by accident or through malevolence, the advances and diffusion of genetic engineering could give rise to unintended, unanticipated diseases, ecological vulnerabilities, and weapons of mass destruction. Dependence on computers, networks and the software that runs them could leave critical parts of society's life-support systems, from nuclear power plants and medical systems to security and sewage treatment facilities, open to both inadvertent yet catastrophic crashes and intentionally debilitating attacks. Less deadly but still pernicious risks might emerge as the spread of information technology makes it easier to violate basic privacy or civil rights and to engage in criminal practices ranging from fraud and theft to illegal collusion.

A second set of purely technological risks involves the possibility of greater vulnerability to system-wide breakdowns in, for example, the air-traffic control infrastructure. Some people fear that as the world becomes more diversified, decentralised and dependent on technology, there will be a higher risk of unmanageable failures in either the physical or social systems that underpin survival. Lastly, the third danger relates to ethics, values and mindsets. Even the initial steps in the long-term development and diffusion of radically innovative technologies such as human cloning or computer-based intelligence (or even life-forms) could pose unusually strong challenges to existing ethical and cultural standards, and put greater burdens on people's tolerance of the unknown and foreign. The risk is that the shock induced by certain technological breakthroughs could end up generating serious social unrest.

Fortunately, the extent to which technology advances and actually poses such threats is fundamentally shaped by forces other than pure scientific feasibility. The emergence of these risks will depend not only on the extent of the actual and perceived dangers of new technologies but also, and crucially, on social and political choices. Such matters, however, lead to the broader debate on the enabling conditions for realising technology's potential.

II. REALISING TECHNOLOGY'S POTENTIAL: THE ENABLING MICRO, MACRO AND GLOBAL CONDITIONS

If the risks can be managed, it is plausible that over the next twenty-five years a panoply of technological advances will vastly improve human welfare as well as help set the world's development on a sustainable course. However, as history demonstrates, the availability of a particular scientific discovery or innovative technology is no assurance that its potential will be extended into useful applications, nor that it will diffuse widely or to those who might use it most productively. Reaping the rewards and reducing the dangers generated by technological advances depend on a complex interaction with underlying economic, social and political conditions. Realising the fruits of socio-technical dynamism demands careful consideration of two dimensions: first, how various socio-economic environments lead to differences in the pace and direction of technological innovation and diffusion; and second, what the implications are of the uses and spread of new technologies for the economy and society.

The framework conditions influencing the rate and distribution of technological advances can be broken down into three general categories: micro, macro and global. Socio-economic factors at the micro level involve, on the one hand, the specific institutional and organisational patterns of families, households, enterprises and government agencies, and on the other, the decisions made by individuals in their roles as members of a household, workers, managers, civil servants or politicians. Macro factors are the overall socio-economic circumstances within which households and enterprises must operate. Here, the general conditions and technological predisposition of product, labour and capital markets are shaped by national monetary, fiscal and regulatory policies that can alter the predictability of borrowing conditions (interest rates), price levels, competitors entering a market and changes in employment rates. Lastly, global framework conditions relate to the management of, for example, the international system of trade, investment and technology flows and planet-wide environmental interdependence. There can be little doubt that the rates at which ideas, technology and competitive pressures diffuse around the globe – not to mention the extent of co-operation to reduce conflict and environmental pollution – will play a major role in determining future socio-technological trajectories.

Micro, macro and global framework conditions can thus be seen as either favouring or impeding technological dynamism. Circumstances where the framework conditions are all favourable to technological dynamism are much more likely to open up the possibility of significant changes in socio-technical patterns. Alternatively, should the framework conditions be more adverse to such change, there is less chance that there will be a break from current economic and social structures. There is no one best formula for encouraging socio-technical dynamism. However, a useful distinction can be made between those framework conditions that are likely to be more supportive of major socio-technical transformations (with potentially strongly positive leaps in society's capacity to address challenges and reap rewards) and those that are more linear and remain entrenched in existing patterns.

A.   Micro-level dynamism and resistance to socio-technical change

The micro level prospects for twenty-first century technologies are mixed. There are a number of changes taking place in the way that firms and households organise work and everyday life that seem conducive to technological innovation and diffusion. On the other hand, there could be an important clash between the radical possibilities opened up by technological change and time-honoured traditions, habits and relationships. Adopting new attitudes, accepting alternative approaches to risk management and equipping people for different decision-making structures is rarely straightforward. The chapter by Meinolf Dierkes, Jeanette Hofmann and Lutz Marz examines these complex and sometimes cyclical processes by looking at the prospects for two important sectors that are at different stages of acceptance and diffusion. One is the mature automotive industry and the other is the booming Internet. A third example is included here to provide an even fuller picture: the transitional health sector.

Beyond Henry Ford

Future prospects for the automotive sector provide a good illustration of the forces that give rise to both dynamism and resistance at the micro level. What were, almost a century ago, the automotive sector's great contributions to technological dynamism – the semi-automated assembly line and the vision of the automobile as a mass consumption item – could well become some of the primary constraints on tomorrow's innovation. Like Frederick Taylor's approach to the time-motion division of labour in the steel industry, Henry Ford's techniques of mass production spread throughout the economy in ways that acted as a catalyst for developing both new production technologies and new products. The combination of more efficient organisation of production with advancing technology provided a massive stimulus to innovation, competition and productivity throughout the economy. Consumers, too, became caught up in this vision of mass production, mass consumption. The household integrated a large range of new products and ways of conducting daily life. This involved not only driving the car to work, to the shopping mall and on the family vacation, but also using washing machines, refrigerators and TVs. The search for solutions to social problems also succumbed to the production methods and product design approaches of the automotive era, with huge mass production, mass consumption public programmes even in health, education and welfare. For many years this was a transformative paradigm that propelled productivity forward and inspired major technological advances.

Within the confines of this automotive vision of production, consumption and mobility, there will continue to be considerable scope for iterative innovation. Competition is likely to continue to press firms to improve products, as will initiatives to address the important problems posed by automotive pollution, congestion, and safety. Major strides will probably occur in the technologies used to power vehicles, co-ordinate traffic and protect drivers. The sector will continue to advance through innovations such as "smart" highways, hybrid electric vehicles, extensions of "lean production" methods and, of course, the computerised car with GPS (satellite-based global positioning system) for navigation and a full range of telecommunications links including Internet-based data, voice and video. However, unless there is movement beyond the automotive paradigm, the opportunities for more radical organisational breakthroughs within the factory, the home and society at large could be missed. For instance, realising the potential to reconfigure where and how people work and live in order to greatly reduce overall environmental carrying costs such as those incurred by current transportation systems will, in all likelihood, require fairly decisive breaks with past socio-technical patterns such as commuting to the workplace and driving to the shopping centre.

Internet futures

In contrast, the Internet could pioneer a significantly different vision of work and society. That vision is rooted in, and hence naturally tends to propagate, a form of organisation embodying a more decentralised responsibility and power structure. One way of grasping how the Internet introduces new possibilities is by comparing it with a conceptually similar but technically different electronic network that is now vanishing: electronic data interchange. EDI took a proprietary approach to connecting enterprises, primarily supply networks in manufacturing and finance, in order to improve co-ordination. Pushed forward in the 1970s and 1980s, these exclusive systems were incompatible between vendors, and tended to be expensive and inflexible. Today, in an amazingly short time, the Internet has eclipsed most proprietary EDI systems.

Internet technology, initially developed through public sector initiative, provides free and open access to a valuable asset, a common standard. A powerful economic imperative is unleashed by the Internet's technology: the increasing returns to scale of both networks and a universal, open set of standards. Collaboration not isolation, extension not restriction – those are the watchwords of the Internet. Indeed, one need only consider the rather sudden enthusiasm with which usually irreconcilable competitors work together to ensure that the Internet becomes a seamless, open space for commerce. National governments and international organisations from the OECD to the W3C (World Wide Web Consortium) are striving to make sure that the Internet becomes a widely shared and level playing field free from obstacles to electronic commerce, e-mail, and the open flow of information.

Compared with the hierarchical, largely centralised models of organisation dominant in most private and public sector places of work (and even in many households), the Internet is an anarchistic, overly decentralised and disorganised (virtual) place. It is an ocean of information connected according to the non-linear rules of hyper-links. It is highly efficient for sharing ideas and taking the initiative to make spontaneous connections oblivious to distance, time zones or preconceptions. It is in marked contrast with the more rigid industrial paradigm of mass production and mass consumption. The Internet thrives in a world where intangible assets are more important than yesterday's fixed assets and digital copying means almost zero-marginal cost reproduction. As a result, the Internet has the potential to transform completely many of the institutional and behavioural patterns that have characterised at the micro level both the supply and demand sides of OECD economies. On the supply side, new forms of work organisation, product development and distribution, market entry and collaboration are emerging. On the demand side, consumption is beginning to shift from passive to active modes. Entirely new business models are being invented in order to exploit these new conditions profitably. Individuals and firms are using the Net not only to actively seek existing products but also to initiate the production of items they conceived. The consumer is beginning to take on a key role formerly reserved for the producer. If this paradigm shift continues to diffuse, there is a chance that across a wide range of activities the value-added chain may be turned upside down.

Sustaining and extending such a radically different culture will take time, and could even fail. True decentralisation of decision-making and co-ordination that goes beyond telework just to save office space and reduce commuting will require individuals to take responsibility throughout the day, from the moment they choose (as producer/consumers) their personally unique breakfast cereal mix to the innovation they dream up (as worker/entrepreneur) in co-operation with a customer that afternoon. This is a daunting challenge. People are naturally resistant to giving up familiar strategies for achieving economic and social success, managing risk and assuring continuity. Although it may at times only be a question of perception, of how someone looks at change – "is it a threat or an opportunity?" – a new paradigm can be very disruptive. The demands of networked "dynamic reciprocity" go well beyond the roles people are trained to perform and the ways of learning that have been fostered by schools, offices and most homes. For all the potential of the Internet paradigm there are many constraints, not least of which is the powerful tendency to reimpose traditional methods by simply grafting the old patterns onto the new. These counter-currents can be seen in all areas, from the private firm or public agency that merely uses the Internet to de-layer operations without changing the organisational culture, to misconceived government policy initiatives that impose industrial era solutions on knowledge economy problems.

Healthcare prospects

Healthcare is already in transition. In most OECD countries the traditional approach to human health leaned heavily on the industrial mass production and mass consumption model, with the hospital as factory and the patient as passive consumer. The paradigm did lead to tremendous gains in reducing the mortality and morbidity associated with disease and accidents. Recently, however, serious limits have emerged in terms of both cost and effectiveness. Reform is under way, with considerable iterative technological and organisational progress already made and even more expected when it comes to controlling costs and improving delivery methods. What is less certain is the extent to which the combination of info- and bio-technologies will actually transform the current medical services sector into a decentralised, active source of preventative maintenance of more than physiological well-being. As indicated earlier, there is a possibility that the breakthroughs expected in understanding genetic and biological processes, along with the power of computing to monitor, store and assess huge quantities of biodata, could lead to major advances in the identification of hereditary and environmental factors likely to affect people's health. This potential for much greater individual control and prevention of health risks could bring with it a redistribution of power and transformation of the institutional and behavioural context. There are, however, many micro-level obstacles to such a transition.

Foremost, perhaps, is the fear and ignorance that still pervade most people's view of their health. The notion of taking personal charge of disease prevention, diagnosis and most treatment is not yet a widely shared vision in today's society. There are ethical and knowledge barriers, but there are also a wide range of institutional and entrenched interests that are likely to oppose a change in the sources of health-related information and decision-making. Here home-based real-time diagnostic and treatment technology, by making health outcomes much more transparent, could play a key role in reducing risks, opening up new markets and enabling institutional and behavioural change. In a world where health information is much more understandable and reliable, individuals can be expected to begin making their own choices. This, in turn, is likely to open up new markets and spur the development of new products that would allow people to benefit from the advances of info- and bio-tech. Technological advances, along with changes to the regulatory systems that protect and concentrate the present patterns of control of health-related information, could turn patients from passive consumers to active controllers. They could also turn medical monopolists into open competitors and doctors themselves into a new breed of practitioner.

Micro-level risks and resistance

Overall, these kinds of radical, technology-enabled changes in the micro-level organisation of work or in the familiar model of passive mass consumption could seriously disrupt or destroy a range of established mechanisms for managing or reducing the costs and risks of organised activity. Some of the most basic assumptions that underpin what people know and expect in the workplace and the home could be called into question. For instance, with the explosive development of technologies such as the Internet, there is likely to be an accelerating trend away from the reassurances, subtle information-sharing and planning assumptions that were once offered by stable career patterns, fixed responsibility pyramids, familiar local shops, and face-to-face encounters at work or in the schoolyard or doctor's office. Continued "dis-intermediation" – a term that refers to the radical changes that occur in the mediating role of the retailer or university when bypassed by the establishment of direct links between the producer and consumer, student and teacher – will in all probability compound the disruption of established micro-level organisational patterns.

Leaving behind the habits of the mass production, mass consumption era will not only overturn numerous comforting firm- and household-level traditions, but also demand the introduction of new mechanisms that are at least as capable of furnishing reliable and inexpensive information and expectations as yesterday's world of top-down orders and standardized choices. Without new methods for reducing risks, the perception of risk, and the costs of acquiring dependable information, socio-technical dynamism will likely slow down. Rapid technological development and diffusion are unlikely to take place without inventiveness, spontaneity and openness on the part of workers and consumers. Successfully addressing these challenges will, in large part, depend on the nature of the changes that take place in the surrounding macro and global framework conditions. These issues are discussed in the next section.

B. Macro- and global-level dynamism and resistance to socio-technical transformation

In general terms, the "conventional wisdom" is that a number of powerful macro and global trends will probably continue to create a fairly positive context for technological progress over the next few decades:

- first, the persistence of widespread adherence to economic policies aimed at non-inflationary growth, structural adjustment and reductions of public deficits and debt;

- second, the continuation of steady growth in productivity as competition drives forward innovation and the accumulation of intangible capital (technical, human and organisational), particularly in the service sectors of developed countries and the industrial sectors of the developing world;

- third, the continued reduction of restraints on market functioning at domestic level through deregulation and privatisation of such sectors as transportation and communication;

- fourth, the further liberalisation of international trade (including services), foreign direct investment and cross-border technology flows;

- and lastly, the ongoing integration of more and more countries, some of them with huge domestic markets, into the global economy.

Taking as given that these basically positive framework conditions will, for the most part, prevail does not resolve the question of the extent to which macro- and global-level conditions will encourage fundamental socio-technical continuity or dynamism. Proceeding along one or the other of these alternative paths will in large part hinge on responses to two further challenges. The first involves the capacity to sustain the positive impact of "knowledge spillovers". What is at stake here are those conditions that either encourage or discourage the high level of information-sharing necessary to spark breakthroughs in socio-technical organisation. The second challenge involves the establishment of an environment that encourages the emergence of new patterns of productive organisation, income, employment, consumption and public-private interaction. Creating these conditions, which not only allow but encourage a high degree of flexibility and innovation throughout society, will play a crucial part in determining the realisation and pace of socio-technical dynamism. Differences in how these two challenges are addressed will constitute a decisive factor in either accelerating or slowing down the emergence of the technological, organisational and structural changes that might, for instance, usher in a new post-automotive Internet era.

Macro

One way of clarifying how different macro-level responses give rise to distinct paths toward socio-technical dynamism is to consider two scenarios of what might happen to the national or regional economies of OECD countries over the next two decades; these are elaborated in the chapter by Emilio Fontela. One scenario depicts a somewhat extreme vision of an almost exclusively market-driven society and the other an equally pushed version of a "new society" model. Neither scenario has a monopoly on socio-technical dynamism. Rather, what emerges is that different approaches to macro-level challenges can be expected to generate distinct sets of impediments and encouragements to socio-technical change.

"Market" scenario

The primary attribute of the Market scenario is a radical reduction of public activities to those of the "night watchman" state which attends only to military, judicial, administrative and regulatory issues. All of the social services, including education, health, social security and welfare, as well as other services such as transportation and communications, are left up to private sector market delivery. The introduction of market discipline to the social services sector is expected to accelerate the pace of innovation, leading to more rapid economic growth. This is in turn likely to lead to a virtuous circle where fully privatised social services can respond to demand with greater output and relative price declines, which then spurs further demand. With booming health, education and insurance sectors in private hands, the fiscal requirements of the public sector should fall, leading to lower interest rates and hence lower capital costs for private investment. The combination of competition-driven technological change and lower capital costs could cause a significant displacement of labour, particularly in the more labour-intensive service sectors such as banking. However, labour market conditions for employment are not expected to deteriorate, since in this scenario wages are sufficiently flexible to achieve full employment. On the downside, there is a good chance that income inequality will widen rapidly, along with the associated problems of exclusion and social costs. A similar accumulation of negative social externalities, items kept outside the purview of minimalist state intervention, could also develop to the point where environmental conditions and general quality of life indicators, *e.g.* infant mortality among the very poor, deteriorate.

The technological dynamism of the Market scenario arises primarily from the powerful competitive forces that are given complete freedom to transform what and how goods and services are produced. A drastic reduction in the constraints that might inhibit technological change leads to significant innovation across all sectors of the economy. At the same time, however, important counter-forces are likely to develop as the degree of uncertainty and insecurity rises. One of the main brakes on the rate and distribution of technological development and diffusion could turn out to be fear of the harsh penalties for failure. In a world of privatised social services, few regulatory requirements and high degrees of income inequality, many people may adopt strategies at work and at home that minimise risk by sticking to what is familiar and more predictable. Macro-level turbulence could induce greater micro-level risk-aversion, thereby slowing down considerably some of the key behavioural changes that are usually essential to the full development and utilisation of technological potential. Another significant constraint on overall dynamism in this scenario would arise if there is a reduction of knowledge spillovers from both the private and public sectors. On the private side, information hoarding and excessive secrecy could combine with highly restrictive treatment of intellectual property to shut down or severely limit the sharing of ideas that is essential for learning and creativity. On the public side, the reduction in government support for both R&D and the delivery of social services could end up eliminating or significantly reducing the free flow of information, a necessary condition for most technological advances. Such an overall increase in the exclusivity of intellectual property might end up crippling both the development and the diffusion of new technologies, and generate seriously negative consequences at the macro level.

"New Society" scenario

The New Society scenario depends, in large measure, on leadership from the public sector in reaping many of the gains from technological development and diffusion. Using public procurement across the full range of government services in conjunction with active support for R&D spurs innovation and the wide diffusion of technologies that serve collectively determined goals. Improving the quality of life and taking steps towards the establishment of an ecologically sustainable society are at the forefront of the technological agenda. Fairly rapid growth of productivity is expected to continue in those sectors exposed to competition, but without market-based imperatives driving technological advances in the social services – and faced with higher financial requirements in the public sector – this scenario shows lower overall economic growth rates. With slower growth and somewhat less flexibility in labour and capital markets there is likely to be a much weaker market-based solution to excess unemployment. Instead, efforts would need to be made to find regulatory and institutional measures to share work hours more equitably among the active labour force, and even to go so far as to redefine and perhaps delink the relationship between income and paid work (e.g. minimum guaranteed income). Complications arise in this scenario from efforts to redesign incentive systems, including taxes, without generating excessive dependency, "moral hazards", protectionism and risk-avoidance. Public sector inefficiencies and sub-optimal resource allocation could also weigh heavily on macro performance in this scenario.

Technological dynamism, however, gains considerable support from the more mission-oriented and open nature of knowledge development and sharing. With clearly articulated public priorities for the health, education, energy, transportation and communication sectors, considerable reorganisation and technical innovation occur. Info- and bio-technology are more explicitly harnessed to a policy agenda and the private sector also faces greater market certainty with regard to innovative efforts in many areas such as learning, medicine, electric power generation, public transit, etc. The pursuit of accessibility targets to ensure broader equality of opportunity seem likely to provide modest incentives for technical innovations aimed at cost reduction and usability improvements. Nevertheless, such incentives would probably fall short of the creative/destructive intensity of wide-open market forces. As a result, technological opportunities are likely to be lost while institutional continuity in the fields of education, social security and labour market regulation leads to inflexibility and complacency. Although for some firms and individuals the micro-level risks that arise when pursuing technological innovation are reduced, for many there is the temptation to continue with business as usual, which could inhibit both the development and adoption of new techniques and ways of organising daily life. These rigidities increase the cost of realising important public policy goals, such as environmental sustainability, that might require considerable restructuring of basic approaches to today's resource-intensive production and consumption. From a macro perspective the New Society model offers both the merits and demerits of an overly stable, preconceived and centralised framework for technology development and diffusion.

Macro-level risks and resistance

Reality will no doubt be less pure than either of these two scenarios. At the macro level of national approaches, two stylised possibilities might be more realistic. One is that in the future the domestic framework moves towards some middle-of-the-road model that is half-hearted in both its efforts to encourage the extension of private markets and its attempt to provide public sector leadership. This grey option could end up with the worst of both worlds, with innovation restrained in both the private and public sectors. A second national-level option moves in the opposite direction by expanding the scope of competitive markets wherever possible while at the same time championing public sector initiatives where they facilitate adaptability, socio-technical dynamism and well-being. This approach would have the virtue of encouraging change at a national level, but might end up generating significant friction at the international level if different countries adopt divergent and inherently incompatible policies.

Either way, socio-technical dynamism could be seriously delayed or misdi-rected by macro-level hurdles arising from the inadequacy of the basic frameworks needed for the smooth functioning of everything from labour and capital markets to intellectual property rights and fundamental scientific research systems. Examples already abound where the spread of the flexible, creative economy has out-stripped the capacity of established employment rules, compe-tition laws, securities regulations, knowledge-sharing incentive schemes (*e.g.* uni-versity funding formulas), and even copyright and patent administrations. Undoubtedly, the nature and extent of these problems will vary across countries in accordance with differences in macro-level framework conditions and the underlying capacity to pursue socio-technical dynamism. In some nations or regions the most acute problems are being posed by anti-competitive practices and the danger that collusion and/or tacit acceptance of technology standards will end up locking in inferior solutions. In other places the main challenges involve adapting labour and capital market regulations and customs to the diverse and often unexpected changes in direction of an innovation-driven economy.

Finally, in either scenario there is the risk that in a more technologically complex and interdependent world the continuation of today's unequal access to and distribution of knowledge would exacerbate the already serious cleavages within society and between regions. Polarisation of technology insiders and out-siders, be it within a city, a region like Europe or across oceans, could end up imposing a range of constraints on socio-technical dynamism. Protectionism, social strife, intolerance and even hatred or open conflict might be inflamed by growing and seemingly unbridgeable gaps between the knowledge haves and have-nots within and between countries. Should such fragmentation, isolation and exclusion proliferate, the pace of socio-technical dynamism would likely be slowed considerably. This in turn might provoke the kind of vicious as opposed to virtuous spiral that ends up further exacerbating problems such as inequality, environmental degradation and global tension.

Global

At the global level there is the possibility of a heterogeneous world where some countries or regions pursue the pure Market model and others the New Society approach. In this context there might be an optimal mix where the advantages of one model are used to fill the gaps of the other. Or, equally plausible, system frictions could arise as the different models have difficulty coexisting. However, before venturing further towards the consideration of the policy issues, it is important to examine the more general question of the relationship of global-level frameworks to socio-technical dynamism and resistance. Here, once again, the focus is on the challenge of establishing the conditions in which "knowledge spillovers" and organisational change are likely to encourage socio-technical transformation. As Luc Soete points out in his contribution to this volume, establishing effective global framework conditions will probably play a decisive role in the development and diffusion of many technological breakthroughs over the next twenty-five years.

Opportunities and risks

Global framework conditions are likely to be critically important for four reasons. First, continued progress towards a seamless global economic system, with harmonized approaches toward, *e.g.*, intellectual property rights, will probably be indispensable for the effective allocation of investments that underpin both technological advances and the infrastructure needed for socio-economic change. Second, it will be difficult for scientific and technical innovators to capitalise on the leverage made possible by advances in information and communications technologies without strong systems for ensuring knowledge openness and sharing on a global basis. Third, in the commercial realm, both the pressures to compete and the capacity to innovate will be deeply influenced by the extent of global information transparency regarding everything from prices and quality standards to market place collusion and differences in tax regimes. And lastly, the ability to devote resources to the general advancement of technology and the human condition will likely depend on the success or failure of efforts to achieve global co-operation regarding planet-wide issues such as environmental pollution, disease, hunger and poverty. In sum, both advancing towards as well as reaping the benefits of tomorrow's ever-"smaller" planet will depend on the establishment of open, transparent and co-operative framework conditions at the global level.

Without addressing the geopolitical aspects of such global frameworks, there are a number of complicating factors that are likely to be pushed forward by the attributes of emerging technological possibilities. Four divisive forces in particular may reduce the chances of establishing conducive global framework condi-

tions. The first involves the values or cultural assumptions that are either premises for or built into particular technologies such as the Internet or genetic
engineering. Here, the risk is that the socio-technical pioneers will ignore the
clash of cultures and insist on market access as if it were value-neutral. This could
lead to confusing legitimate, democratically expressed social preferences for protectionism, thereby invoking possibly harmful international tensions. The second
difficult issue for global frameworks involves the new burdens presented by the
destructive potential of some socio-technical possibilities – including easier
access to the knowledge needed to attain lethal military or terrorist capacity and
greater vulnerability of key infrastructures to attack over the Internet. More than
ever, it will be crucial to assess and monitor at a global level the dangers, even if
inadvertent, that might arise in an environment that is conducive to socio-
technical dynamism. Third, there is the particular risk that today's global
frameworks may be more vulnerable to fragmentation as socio-technical advances
allow effective decision-making to descend towards the local and ascend towards
the global simultaneously. In this context, differences might be exacerbated and
the crucially important global agreements could either disintegrate or fail to
emerge. Lastly, the power of technology and new forms of organisation could work
to undermine the effectiveness and legitimacy of important collective institutions,
from the centralised firm and national government to the family and religious
organisations. The current base of the pyramid upon which global frameworks rest
could begin to crumble as socio-technical dynamism disrupts existing patterns of
assuring societal cohesion.

All of these tensions are amply illustrated by the challenge of achieving
environmental sustainability in the next century.

The example of environmental sustainability

Environmental sustainability offers one of the best examples of the divergent
implications of realising (or not) global frameworks conducive to socio-technical
transformation. The first reason is that socio-technical progress is probably an
indispensable part of improving ecological outcomes without facing unacceptable
trade-offs in terms of wealth or individual liberty. Secondly, environmental
sustainability is the foremost example of two sets of externalities: the cross-
jurisdictional nature of pollution, and the probability that the overall social rates
of return on investments in socio-technical change aimed at improving the environment are greater at a global level than at the country level.

Unlike certain previous technological challenges – such as the Manhattan
Project, which resolutely pursued the major scientific and engineering breakthroughs needed to build an atomic bomb in the utmost secrecy and isolation –
the success of efforts to achieve environmental sustainability will depend largely

on the capacity to openly share and jointly develop socio-economic and technological changes. Similarly, it will be important, as noted above, to seek global framework conditions that are sensitive to the cultural, educational and income differences that may inhibit the worldwide development and diffusion of the socio-technical change. This is not just a challenge for developing countries. For example, making the leap to less wasteful and more local energy production and consumption will probably require fairly radical breaks from existing patterns of working and living, and from the passive and highly resource-intensive approaches, that now largely predominate in most OECD countries.

As for the externalities associated with the global environment, they clearly indicate the need to push global co-operation to new levels. A case in point is the shift to much greater use of local renewable energy sources: progress in this field is likely to require a wide range of often disruptive, expensive and mutually contingent initiatives. For instance, decentralisation of power generation and management to the household and firm level, reversing a century-long tradition of centralisation, would probably involve major reorientations in energy research and product development, significant regulatory changes, major educational efforts, new energy pricing/cost structures, complex equity considerations, and probably lifestyle adaptation. Waiting for one jurisdiction to take on all of the learning costs associated with such a paradigm transition would probably lead to sub-optimal delays from the perspective of the global social returns to be gained from wide diffusion. Competitive forces such as those being unleashed in California that lead private utilities to push ahead with the offer of solar power options to customers will play an important and positive role. But given the technical and equity challenges associated with the conversion to sustainable energy patterns, it will probably be necessary to share costs and benefits at a global level. Without such sharing there is a good chance that the social and technological changes needed to achieve sustainability will either fail to occur or emerge very slowly.

Towards a global approach to encouraging socio-technical dynamism

Ultimately, in light of increasing international interdependence, global as opposed to national-level approaches look set to become the most effective way of addressing macro-level problems such as ensuring that stocks and bonds can be traded seamlessly worldwide, or that producers of intellectual property are compensated fairly and efficiently when someone uses their output. Indeed, one of the main macro-level obstacles to socio-technical dynamism is the fact that available institutions are national or inter-nation(al) while many emerging challenges appear to require more holistic, global thinking. As many analysts have pointed out, particularly with respect to future environmental sustainability, the shift towards more integrated, planet-wide initiatives will probably accelerate as people come to recognise the enhanced benefits – both private and social – of action at a global level.

Finally, converging economic, social and technological forces seem poised to create a leap in both the importance and feasibility of global management. From this vantage point, overcoming the obstacles to socio-technical dynamism serves simultaneously as a catalyst to address the challenges likely to be posed by greater interdependence and as a way of developing the tools needed to tackle such global issues. These linkages flow naturally to consideration of the most promising directions for policies aimed at stimulating socio-technical dynamism while minimising the risks and overcoming the varied and often complex barriers.

III. MAKING THE MOST OF 21st CENTURY TECHNOLOGIES: STRATEGIES FOR ENCOURAGING SOCIO-TECHNICAL DYNAMISM

Many people welcome the prospect of technological innovation offering such bountiful possibilities for the twenty-first century. However, along with this optimism there is also a profound recognition that both the desirability and feasibility of technological developments will depend primarily on the introduction and diffusion of numerous economic, social and governmental enabling conditions. Reciprocally, the direction, pace and diffusion of scientific innovation is seen as fundamentally influencing the underlying structures of knowledge, economic incentives and social constraints. Thus, the realisation of technology's potential will, it is widely accepted, depend in large part on encouraging a complex interaction of mutually reinforcing societal and technological advances – an interplay that can be called socio-technical dynamism.

Four particularly potent and pervasive forces can be identified as prime factors likely to spur the advance of socio-technical dynamism over the next few decades. First, the diffusion and intensification of competition in existing and emerging markets locally, regionally and globally seem set to provide an important stimulus to all forms of technological and organisational innovation. Second, the transition to a knowledge economy promises to both rupture entrenched relationships of the industrial era and open up new horizons for intangible, non-firm-based value-added activity. In tomorrow's networked knowledge economy, imagination – even artistry – may become as important as the increasingly vital competitive edge gained by being first to market with a new product. Third, growing economic, social and environmental interdependence, particularly at the global level, will probably compel significant changes in the way knowledge, resources and sovereignty are managed. And fourth, undiminished individual and collective aspirations – people's hopes for a better life – are also likely to play a major role in both altering public policy parameters and leading individuals to take the risk of adopting new patterns for structuring the where, when and how of many basic human activities.

Each of these strong currents could be expected to generate significant economic and social changes; combined, they are likely to furnish a powerful wave upon which socio-technical dynamism will move into the twenty-first century. Just as the transition from agriculture to industry opened up a vast range of new choices for firms, individuals and governments, so too could socio-technical dynamism and the transition to a knowledge-based economy and society. Barring catastrophic political breakdown or natural disasters that could freeze the status quo, it is broadly expected that a dynamic socio-technical path will generate changes in the basic conditions of life for most people. For businesses and households in OECD countries, taking a dynamic socio-technical path will probably mean breaking with a wide range of ingrained habits and customs in order to move towards unprecedented levels of proactive innovation and customisation in all aspects of commerce and life. In much of the rest of the world, the changes could be equally dramatic as new forms of industrial organisation and technology diffuse more fully. Over the course of the next few decades it is not far-fetched to expect major transformations in the long-established patterns of where people work, what they produce, when they engage in learning activity, how they structure different phases of their life and day, what they consume, who supplies them, and how they interact.

Fostering such socio-technical dynamism over the next few decades will demand an emphasis on two broad goals. First, decision-makers in both the public and private sectors will need to devote considerable effort to encouraging individual and organisational creativity – the capacity and liberty to introduce innovations and changes into the ways in which we work and live. Second, in the public and private domain there will need to be substantial stress on ways of improving collective decision-making at the local, national and (perhaps most importantly) global level in order both to advance socio-technical dynamism and to reap and share its benefits. Much of the analysis stresses the strong interdependence between co-operative efforts to ensure the accessibility and reliability of information in the knowledge economy, and the individual capacity to compete, assess risk and learn. Equally interdependent are the co-operative pursuits of openness, tolerance, and people's ability to find creative inspiration in the free sharing of ideas and contrasting perspectives.

Highlighting these two goals for future policy does not in any way imply an abandonment of more familiar policy thrusts, such as ensuring a stable macroeconomic framework; encouraging structural adjustment through flexible product, labour and capital markets; improving people's learning capacity; and preventing social exclusion. On the contrary, rather than diminishing in importance, these well-known policy priorities are seen by most analysts as crucial for achieving the creativity and co-operation underpinning an innovative, adaptable economic and social context. A stable macroeconomic framework – consisting of policies that aim for low inflation and solid public sector finances – plays a key role in reducing some of the volatility that can discourage risk-taking and innovation. More flexible labour markets, transparent and open capital markets, and competitive goods and services markets are all essential to the fluid resource reallocation and experimentation that are likely to be typical of robust socio-technical dynamism. Another continuing policy priority will involve adapting the learning infrastructure – including but not limited to the industrial era's preoccupation with the educational supply side and massive R&D projects – to the requirements of an innovative knowledge economy. Ongoing efforts will also be needed to make sure that social support, pension and healthcare systems are adapted in ways that correspond to the needs of tomorrow's highly diverse, possibly less predictable society. Taken as a whole, the reforms currently under way in these conventional policy areas are likely to be necessary although not sufficient for fostering socio-technical dynamism in the twenty-first century.

Meeting the challenge of nurturing an innovation-driven economy and society will likely require equally inventive policy initiatives. For many commentators there will probably need to be a major overhaul of competition and intellectual property laws and administration to take into account the greater importance of intangible assets and global markets. The Internet's extra-national characteristics will also demand novel policy responses. New ground will have to be broken in order to provide the policy frameworks that enable existing technologies to provide every person with the verifiable cyberspace identity needed for voting or sharing medical data. Breakthroughs will also probably be needed in managing global issues like climate change and in pursuing the development and diffusion of technologies that ease some of the negative trade-offs between economic growth and environmental sustainability while at the same time capitalising on the possible synergies. As micro-level decentralisation alters the mass production/mass consumption paradigm, new forms of risk-sharing, information verification and spontaneous co-operation will need to emerge. Rules – in some cases, creative regulatory initiatives – regarding electronic commerce will probably be essential for encouraging both the global functioning of existing markets such as insurance or equities, and the development of entirely new transactions such as the sale to business database services of private personal information (*e.g.* individual preferences, income, purchasing intentions, evaluations of products or brands).

Less typical issues will also need to be integrated into the policy mix. In many cases, sparking transformations in values and culture will be an essential part of facilitating the necessary tolerance of new ideas and diverse lifestyles, as well as entrepreneurialism and experimentation. Pursuing these goals will require a wide range of inventive policies with particular sensitivity to local, national and regional differences. Finding the appropriate combinations of public and private, local and global, innovative and traditional approaches will be not only an ongoing challenge but also a moving target. For if creativity is to be the well-spring of progress, then the conditions that assure such socio-technical dynamism are likely to be continuously evolving.

THE NEXT TWENTY-FIVE YEARS
OF TECHNOLOGY: OPPORTUNITIES AND RISKS

by

Joseph Coates
Coates & Jarratt, Inc., United States

Looking ahead a quarter-century to the practical developments in and applications of technology is not as difficult as many people think. A good number of technologies now coming into use will take years or even decades to reach the point of significant consequence for society. On the other hand, the history of technology in the industrial era tells us that it is usually fifteen to forty years from the time of a fundamental scientific discovery to its effective application in society. Attending to what is now emerging and also looking at the fundamental developments in science can provide insights into technology's future. Before turning to those specifics, there are a half-dozen concepts which relate to the choice and depth of application of new developments.

First, the biggest risk that we face is the failure to embrace the potential that new technologies offer for improving the condition of humankind and the state of nations.

Second, and closely related, is the risk of over- or underregulation, and over- or undercapitalisation of new developments. Either can thwart the desirable or fail to constrain the undesirable.

Third, the most common error in forecasting is that of the enthusiast who is so optimistic about a new development that he or she neglects the social, economic and political constraints, and anticipates the arrival of the new technology far sooner than it can occur.

Fourth, the complement of that error is to overlook the secondary effects of new technology. The side-effects often are more significant than the basic problems meant to be solved by the technology's introduction. Virtually all technologies are introduced on the basis of substitution. They do something better, cheaper, sooner or more reliably, or have some other microeconomic benefit. In capitalistic societies that introduction is largely brought about through a buyer/

seller chain in which there is little incentive to look at the longer-term consequences or side-effects of the new technology. For example, when the word processor was brought into office life there was little awareness beyond the introduction of an improved tool for secretarial work. No one recognised that two consequences would be, first, a substantial diminution in the size of the secretarial staff, and second, the phenomenon of professional workers themselves adopting the tool and reducing the need for that external support.

Fifth, the boundless cornucopia of technologies is producing too many choices for business, for government, for industry and for consumers. Those choices may range from a new variation on a portable cassette player to alternative sources of energy in a province of a developing country. The risk is that of basing decisions not on future outcomes but rather on the short-term, local, and too often self-serving forces reflecting immediate concerns.

Sixth, the world is too complex to be contained within one single category. It is more useful to consider that there are three worlds. World 1 is the advanced nations: Europe, the United States, Canada, Australia, New Zealand, and Japan. World 2 is nations where needs and resources are in rough balance and where most of the rapid economic development is now occurring. World 3 refers to those countries – Bangladesh and Nigeria are examples – that are in severe straits with no clear path to a positive future. As a consequence, technology will not be uniform in its effects. The likely flow in most cases will be from World 1 to 2 to 3. On the other hand many of the choices that will be made in World 3 will reflect not the high income and consumer orientation of World 1 but rather the realities of government dealing with the basic necessities of food, clothing, shelter, sanitation and transportation.

In looking at the technological material discussed below, the reader is invited to consider the above six underlying concepts in relation to each new development.

Not since the beginning of the Industrial Revolution have the prospects for technologies benefiting mankind been so bright. In the advanced nations all people live in a totally man-made world. The devices, artefacts, materials and systems of society are all products of the engineering enterprise. Even remote places are likely to be under the watchful eye of government backed by a hi-tech support and rescue system. The rest of the world is steadily moving toward the same condition.

Globalisation of world economies, through promotion of international trade and commerce, is creating a global division of labour among all nations. Ultimately everything in commerce will be raw materials grown or mined through highly engineered technologies, manufactured products, or advanced services dependent upon engineered systems. Even those aspects of human enterprise which are closest to raw nature – agriculture and animal husbandry – are increasingly technologised. Their steadily rising productivity depends upon technology-based systems. The story of farming and its high productivity in World 1 is well known. Animal husbandry is producing the industrially managed and engineered chicken and hog; beef is not far behind.

The "big" forces of nature – weather, tides, earthquakes and volcanic eruptions – are better understood, as a result of complex engineering systems for data-gathering, analysis, interpretation and forecasting. We are on the brink of engineered interventions to influence and even control these fundamental forces of nature.

As our technologised world moves towards a complexity unprecedented in history and largely unanticipated in the early and middle phases of the industrial era, technology itself becomes more complex. The scientist or engineer, to be more successful in the future, is likely to be hyphenated – that is, to have training in two or more fields and to draw them together as his or her special competency. Competency implies that the end of school and beginning of a career is only a way station in lifelong intellectual refurbishment and the ongoing acquisition of new skills. While the traditional categories of engineering in the world of practical applications are melding, the universities are laggard in that they continue to stick too closely to those categories – civil, electrical, electronic, chemical, mechanical and science (chemistry, physics, biology, etc.).

Applied science is often just another form of technology or engineering, while engineering draws upon the newest developments in science. For example, the computer – coming out of basic scientific developments, reduced to practice by engineers and continually improved by both – has become a transformational tool of the contemporary world. At the same time, it is now reflexively opening all technological areas to undreamed-of skills in planning, design, execution, monitoring, test and evaluation.

Some areas of engineering will clearly flourish in the early decades of Millennium 3. In a three-year project, Coates & Jarratt, Inc. collected all of the forecasts in all of the areas of science, engineering and technology that could be found, from around the world. These were analysed in a systematic way, and 41 reports running to about 4 000 pages were produced. Later, in the second phase of the project, we produced our own forecast for the year 2025, which has now been published as a book.* In that panoramic examination of expectations from science and engineering, it was clear that six areas of new developments would be

* Joseph F. Coates, John B. Mahaffie and Andy Hines (1997), *2025: Scenarios of US and Global Society Reshaped by Science and Technology*, Oak Hill Press, Greensboro, North Carolina.

fundamental shapers of the next stages of the human enterprise. The great enablers will be:

- genetics technology;
- energy technology;
- materials technology;
- brain technology;
- information technology.

A sixth area, not itself a technology but acting as an influential wash over all technologies, will be environmentalism.

As each new development of science matures it is refined into effective technological applications through engineering. Genetics for example will, as the human genome project comes to completion, lead to technologies of diagnosis and evaluation of individuals' potential diseases or shortfalls in capabilities. Everyone will have for themselves and their children, and at low cost, an implicit picture of their likely personal development or evolution. That will create a new boom in medical technologies as means of intervention are sought to correct, neutralise or modify undesirable conditions and ultimately to genetically enhance ourselves. The technologies for collecting, organising, interpreting and dealing with that knowledge will create information networks and radically improve epidemiology.

Combining the technologies of data-mining with the availability of health smart cards (brain on a chip) or universal health and medical information networks, new means will be engineered to identify the external and internal origins of human diseases and disorders.

The technologies for manipulating other living things will be more drastic and, in many regards, more effective. New technologies for controlling pests, for enhancing food sources, for expanding and manipulating biota, for rapidly creating new plant varieties and new transgenic species will all expand the capacity for healthful survival on an increasingly congested and integrated planet.

GENETICS TECHNOLOGY

In the past fifty years it has been established beyond question that the heritable characteristics of all living things are transmitted by a specific class of chemicals called deoxyribonucleic acid, DNA. The DNA consists of four components that are arranged in different patterns which comprise a code. That code in turn allows the DNA programme to create from the material in its cellular environment the specific class of proteins – enzymes – which in turn move on to create everything else to make the organism, whether a micro-organism or a human being, a butterfly or a pine tree. We have over the past half-century learned to decode DNA, how to take it apart, put it back together, synthesise it, even how to combine DNA from different sources or species. We have learned that the DNA characteristics or behaviour coded for will be expressed – that is, will show up in the organism – if the environmental conditions of the organism are appropriate. We have also learned that there are few things more democratic in the universe: DNA from any part of the living kingdom will, when moved into any other part of the living kingdom, in all likelihood express its characteristics if the environment permits it.

The contraceptive technology developed in the earlier decades of this century have separated procreation from recreation. The developments in genetics promise to go further and separate fertilization from the propagation of undesirable characteristics. There are about four thousand human diseases and disorders that are genetically based. They range from some which are a person's absolute destiny if he or she carries them, to others which are only matters of probability, leaving individuals susceptible to certain conditions on exposure to an adverse environment. As we learn more about the genetic basis of individual diseases, constituencies will develop for more research directed at their condition. There will be a flourishing of approaches to preventing, correcting and mitigating the effects of adverse genes. Organisations of people with particular disorders will not only affect government allocation of research but will also influence research in the private sector. If companies are not seen to be putting enough money into a particular disorder, the tools developed by public interest groups – boycotts, propaganda campaigns – will force them into line.

How genetics will affect human choices is most clear in the case of a potentially deadly gene. Diagnosis will establish that one does or does not carry that gene. If one carries it, choices regarding what to do about starting a family will become clearer. First will be the examination of the fetus in utero. If it carries the defect, the choice is most likely to be to abort, less likely to attempt to accommodate and plan for the defective child, and least likely to do nothing and attribute the condition to divine will. But beyond that will be fertilization in the Petri dish. The examination of the fertilized egg after two or three divisions to four or eight cells will be made, and if free of the disorder, implantation can occur and a child can be born free of that disease. The cost of this is extremely high today, but technology will bring that down to acceptable practice over the years.

Lying beyond the dealing with diseases and disorders that is the focus of current government programmes around the world is the inevitable opportunity to move to human enhancement. We are the first generation to be able to intervene in our own evolution.

For over a decade we have been saying that mastodons will walk the earth again, that passenger pigeons will fill the sky, and that the dodo will once again waddle on the island of Mauritius. Every museum is a repository of species ready to be revived by new genetic engineering technologies. The recent breakthrough with Dolly pioneers the use of somatic cells, as opposed to germinal cells, to produce whole healthy animals. Still-edible mastodon flesh is found in Siberia. Surely some of that is in good enough condition that with the technologies developed with Dolly, it will soon be possible to remove an egg from an elephant and replace its nucleus with the activated DNA from the mastodon, and then reimplant it in the elephant. Then eighteen to twenty-two months later the world will have its first living mastodon in 10 000 years.

The effects of genetics on agriculture are virtually boundless. There are about 3 500 edible plants. Some 300 are eaten, about 60 are in commerce, about 30 widely consumed, and about six supply 90 per cent of human nutrition. Most of those left out of the human diet are eliminated because of defects: too much energy required to cook, too much husk, bad smell, undesirable taste, or other characteristics. Direct genetic intervention should influence our diet by expanding the range of things edible. Transgenic plants – plants taking the DNA from distinctly different species and combining them into new products – are just around the corner. We are already seeing the application of the new genetics primarily directed at increasing productivity, surely a desirable short-term economic goal. Ahead of that will be the modification of plants for nutritional improvement. Take the Mexican diet, which is based on rice and beans. Both foods supply protein; neither on its own supplies a balanced diet of protein, yet together they do. In the very near future rice and beans will each be genetically manipulated to provide a totally balanced protein mix. Genetics will go beyond that however, and allow us to modify plants or create new plants, transgenic species, that will thrive in arid zones, in dry climates, in brackish water, and in other environments normally thought of as marginal to unusable.

The application of genetics to micro-organisms is likely to be profoundly important in many regards. Micro-organisms in their democratic acceptance of DNA from any other species are already able to produce large quantities of very complex molecules, too expensive or even too difficult to manufacture by traditional means. But apart from these specialty chemicals, micro-organisms hold the potential for becoming effective competitors for commodity chemicals. A characteristic of every species is that it cannot do anything that its DNA does not permit. Micro-organisms are mostly programmed by their DNA to operate at modest temperatures and pressures, and are capable of producing only specific things. Unlike a chemical plant which, if the temperature rises, produces undesirable and often toxic by-products, micro-organisms will simply stop producing where conditions go awry. Micro-organism-based production of commodity chemicals will be a techno-economic trade-off with alternative ways of production, but it does hold the promise of an unprecedented degree of purity in bulk chemicals and hence fewer environmental concerns.

ENERGY TECHNOLOGY

Engineering has brought us highly effective and economically productive and beneficial dependencies on successive waves of energy sources: first water, then coal, later petroleum, now natural gas, and to a significant degree nuclear power. In the future there will be less dependency on single sources and greater dependency on multiple sources. The one greatest uncertainty in the energy future is whether greenhouse warming due to technological activities will prove to be both real and significant. While it will probably be both, that remains to be established beyond reasonable doubt. If it is, technology will be called on initially and in the short run to deal with the goal of massive energy conservation. The improvement in structures, buildings, design, and insulation with regard to efficient electricity flow (probably through the applications of superconductor materials), and the development of new, more efficient engines using petroleum and natural gas, will all move ahead rapidly and simultaneously. But that will not be enough.

In the future our global energy infrastructure is likely to be structured around two primary sources of noncarbon fuels. One is nuclear power, based largely on the French model, with uniformity of design, economy of scale, and interchangeable parts and staff. The other is solar energy, whose primary contribution will be photovoltaics for direct generation of electricity and passive solar for the production of hot water. Another likely source is wind: great improvements in that technology have developed over the past five years.

The re-engineering of the global energy infrastructure is inevitable should greenhouse-based warming prove, as expressed above, both real and significant. Should it turn out not to be significant, the improved exploitation of fossil fuels will challenge technology. New means of petroleum extraction – what, for lack of a better terminology, could be called quaternary recovery – will emerge depending upon improved geological subsurface mapping, more flexible drilling, and techniques yet to be invented. Natural gas is being found in abundance, and frequently. Finally, and in even greater quantities than petroleum and natural gas, there are the gas hydrates, complexes on the molecular scale of ice cages capturing methane molecules. Engineering is the means by which present and new fuel resources will be optimally discovered or recovered, developed and used.

Policy crises arising from greenhouse warming are now coming into view. The root problem is one of disbelief on the part of the world's policy community, if belief can be measured by the willingness to take effective action. That disbelief is overriding necessary choices – and some viable alternatives.

The clearest strategy to follow with regard to potential greenhouse warming – since its evolution is roughly on the same time frame as the lifetime of a new energy infrastructure, thirty to forty years – would be to promote all those technologies that would have benefits in their own right at little or no cost. Examples might include a hundred-mile-per-gallon automobile, more effective insulation of buildings, long-term investments in unconventional resources such as geothermal energy, or a truly accelerated push in the direction of photovoltaics.

Europe has made the most progress in energy conservation. The United States and Canada lag conspicuously behind, but the real emerging problem lies in neither of those regions but in China, India, and Indonesia; all of the latter countries are opening up to major economic development which, as it now stands, is and will continue to be based on fossil fuels. The global policy issue is to convert that basis to non-carbon alternatives.

MATERIALS TECHNOLOGY

Materials technology is the hidden revolution. Historically, we have been dependent upon the inherent limitations of materials in whatever we build, whether those were limitations of limestone and granite in older structures, or the characteristics of wood over the centuries, or the unique varieties of concrete, or the alloys of steel, brass and aluminum. Each of those sets of characteristics limited what could be done, whether we were making large structures or engineering new products for business, industry or the home. Fundamental new knowledge now allows us to realistically consider designing new materials from scratch with any set of characteristics we choose. Glass, let us say, that is flexible in a certain temperature regime, photoresponsive and perhaps even simultaneously electrically conductive is not beyond our capabilities. Aside from characteristics that would be essentially contradictory – simultaneously wet and dry – we have the capability of at least initiating the exploration to develop any desired characteristics in materials. Once those characteristics are available they become the new material for stimulating engineering creativity and design.

Social forces are acting to push many of the large artefacts of society toward greater durability and longer lifetime, and promoting greater use of recycling, reclamation and remanufacturing. Environmental pressures, limitations on resources, and the capabilities of engineering will make durability and those three Rs universal and routine throughout the world.

Another aspect of materials is the movement to miniaturisation and modularity. Small modules use less material and energy and lend themselves to convenient replacement and centralised repair or reclamation. Miniaturisation, however, is moving well beyond devices one might hold in the palm of one's hand or balance on the top of a fingernail. Micro devices smaller than the cross-section of a human hair are now in commerce. Those devices will function as sensors, actuators, and functioning elements in boundless applications in machines, and in living beings (including people) as measuring instruments and controls. Beyond micromachines lies the more speculative nano world of devices three orders of magnitude smaller than the micro world. The nano world concept depends upon the manipulation of individual atoms and molecules. Nature knows how to do this. It can convert raw material into a protoplasm and then into a plant or animal. The goal of nanotechnology, in the extreme, is by analogy to duplicate with technology what nature does. While it is hardly conceivable that we can collapse 3 billion years of evolution into a few decades, we are already witnessing the engineering ability to cut, to machine, to make sandwiches at the nano level. Those capabilities will develop into important parts of the engineered world over the next decades.

Nature produces materials far more complex, and in many regards more effective, than anything that we can produce technologically. The material from which feathers are made can provide warmth, the shedding of water, and the structures to fly, all of which have to do with different modes of forming the material through the birds' natural processes. Some plants and animals have senses outside our current scope. Some animals use adhesives which should be the envy of industrial processes. Biomimetics, the development of materials in imitation of or analogous to natural products, is another emerging avenue in the materials revolution.

BRAIN TECHNOLOGY

The 1990s in the United States are the decade of the brain. More knowledge has been generated about the structure, function, organisation and operation of the brain during the 90s than in the previous hundred years of scientific exploration. As scientists learn to map and understand the systems of the brain, it would be foolish to attempt to estimate how far we have come in that exploration, but results are produced on a daily basis. It is now clear that many brain or mental functions are site-specific and fundamentally biochemical in nature. As those processes are explored, there are obvious questions. What is the chemistry? If something goes wrong, what causes that? Is this source endogenous? Is that source something we take in from our food, through our skin, or in our breath? If the answers are yes, then how do we intervene to neutralise the bad or enhance the good? These are the basic brain technology questions that will be answered over the next decades. One could take the available knowledge of the whole body and couple that with the emerging knowledge of the brain and come to the realistic conclusion that we will move not merely into a world of corrective medicine, but into one in which the body and the mind will be the unified field of operation for radical cosmetics. No aspect of the human being, whether physical, mental, intellectual, social, psychological or physiological, will be beyond practical manipulation and change, all of which will be made possible and practical through technology.

Consider kleptomania, the compulsive need to steal what one could afford to buy. For most of our lives we have considered it more of a moral defect than anything else, a matter of counselling or punishment or behaviour change. Recently the biochemical site on the brain which is the source of kleptomania has been identified. The condition is without question the result of a biochemical lesion. Identifying that site and that it is a lesion alters our view of what previously was considered a character defect. New knowledge opens up the promise of direct intervention to cure the condition. Every mental characteristic, whether it is a matter of personality, cognition or emotionality, will eventually be identified as a biochemical process which itself is largely genetically determined and hence a candidate for intervention. Those interventions may be pharmaceutical or they may be genetic, acoustic, visual, or by means yet to be developed. A substantial step in the direction of brain technology is the current popularity of the drug Prozac, which was developed to deal with depression. So far it is the closest approach to Aldous Huxley's soma, the "feel good" drug. It has in just a few years become one of the most widely sold drugs in the United States.

The demand is there for mental improvement and enhancement, and the technologies are just beginning to emerge. Within the next decade schizophrenia and psychotic depression will be history in World 1, as the fundamental physiology, genetics and biochemistry are worked out and the appropriate cures – or, more importantly, preventative strategies – are developed. Brain technology will go well beyond disease, offering relief for the person who is short-tempered, the person who has no sense of humour, the person who is overly emotional. And relief from these conditions will itself find a substantial market. Beyond that will be the possibility and later the practice of enhancing people's cognitive processes, enabling them to think more clearly, to have better command of arithmetic, to have a better memory for faces, to be more generous and loving, or to be less prideful or slothful.

INFORMATION TECHNOLOGY

Information technology has already worked radical changes in world society, but we have barely begun to feel the transformational consequences of the newest developments. Fibre optics will in many parts of the world drop the cost of telecommunications so low that it will be virtually free. From a business or a personal point of view, cost will no longer be a consideration in communication. Wireless communication will in itself be of value and will also be a primary flow into and out of the fibre optics network. Low-cost communication will continue to alter radically the way we do business, where we work, and how we work. It will lead to the emergence of electronic commerce and create new systems of relationships while raising new social issues, primarily having to do with equity and privacy. To a substantial degree the answer to those social problems will lie in the way the networks and complex relationships are engineered, designed and regulated. As technology tied to information increases in economic competence it is inevitable and natural that the government will in some way make it a source of revenue. We anticipate a system that will tax the number of bits and bytes, not content. As the cost of telecommunications drops, the important technological opportunities will be less in the network itself and more in end-use applications.

Other unfolding IT developments include the continued growth in computer capacity and speed, and shrinkage in size. The important consequence of those three factors coming together is that every time we increase the capacity by one or two orders of magnitude, we are able to engage a new social problem in real-time management. The traditional approach to a troublesome situation is to examine it, gather data, come to some conclusions, propose changes, make the changes, and then cycle through again. That cycle takes a year. The ability to do real-time management holds the exciting potential of making every system into a continuous open-ended experiment. The importance of that lies not just in the implied technical elegance. As our world becomes more complex, the top decision-makers in business and government are simply unable to make adequate judgements about the management of their complex systems. Yet, given the need to manage, open-ended continuous experimentation is a healthy alternative to making definitive rigid, and often defective, decisions.

Everything will become smart as it acquires its own sensors, microprocessors and actuators – or intrinsically smart, as in the case of some light-responsive glasses. As things become smart through information technology, they will be able to do three things: evaluate their internal performance, evaluate their external performance, and, if either is not good, initiate repair or call for help. Ubiquitous smartness implies, as the next logical step, linking these smart things into systems for more effective and often remote management. It will be commonplace to evaluate, manage and control systems such as an official building or waterworks from a few miles to thousands of miles away.

The engineers who design food packaging will get together with the engineers who design kitchen appliances, and make those food packages as smart as the appliances, and interactive with them. The resulting synergy is likely to cut meal preparation time to a few minutes, programme the system for the various tastes of people who are going to enjoy the meal, and drastically shorten cleanup and maintenance time.

Smartness will show up in many other ways. Homes and buildings have been widely written about as opportunities for smartness, *i.e.* for sensing air leaks, water leaks, break-ins and a score of other things. But smartness in structures will go beyond that. In combining developments in materials with the developments in information technology, an entirely new engineering paradigm for buildings begins to appear. Historically, all buildings have been based upon either compression or tension. The near future could see featherweight buildings in which the support structure, the frame, is made out of high-performance recyclable composites. As the structure is put up it will be laced with steel cables attached to motors. The steel cables will give strength to the structure. External and internal sensors will evaluate the stresses on the building and orchestrate the motors' tension and relaxation in an appropriate way. The emerging paradigm is dynamic, responsive structures. Going a step further, it should be clear that once it is possible to design dynamic buildings, it should be easy to design buildings that are dismantleable and capable of being moved to another site, capable of being made bigger or smaller, taller or shorter as needs change. The way to think about smartness is to take any element, device, system or component of our world, and ask what would it be like when it can do the three functions above that define smartness.

Rapidly reaching parity with telecommunications and computational capabilities are various forms of imaging, from the barcode to virtual reality. Certainly the latter, with or without an assist from other artificial intelligence (AI), will have dramatic technological consequences, not least in the area of education and training. The system will be able to achieve the three historic unmet goals of general education: to combine what is it we wish to pour into the student with what exactly he or she knows now, and fit that with the students' preferred learning strategies – visual, acoustic, kinesthetic, etc. The system will continually optimise to facilitate learning. Tasks that would normally take years will be reduced to weeks or at most months, and tasks that would normally take months to learn could be reduced to days or a couple of weeks. That kind of teaching will for the first time make it possible to have 100 per cent learning for everyone. Virtually every student, in every discipline, at every level of education finds satisfaction if they are getting an 85 or 90 or 98 per cent in their examinations, which means reciprocally that 2, 10 or 15 per cent of the material was not mastered. Virtual reality and AI systems will permit and encourage 100 per cent mastery, which should dramatically affect the lives and careers of those so educated.

Design of all sorts is now being done in cyberspace. The state of that art is developing rapidly; eventually, everything from a can opener to a chemical plant will be tested, evaluated and modified in cyberspace before any physical or solid thing is dealt with. This applies not just to mechanical things, but also to areas such as chemical engineering and even carrying back to molecular design with a specialist, the molecular engineer.

The computer and associated imagery will be dynamic, three dimensional, and multimedia. Ultimately that imagery will not just affect how well we think; it will change the ways we think, cultivating mental processes that are pictorial, multidimensional and dynamic.

Information will come together in many different ways to create new applications. Consider for example the next time the president or prime minister of a democracy is to speak. Engineers will design a network of 10 000 homes to get a fair sample; while 1 200 would do it, the public will have more confidence in 10 000. As the president is giving his talk, the 10 000 people will be asked to respond on a scale of one to five about whether they agree or disagree with what is being said. As he speaks, histograms will appear over the president's left shoulder. The number 1 could mean "damn lie", 5 "agree completely". That kind of political dynamite could blow away the empty rhetoric and encourage cognitive content in political discourse. Imagine the same capability engineered into every business as well as government, for all kinds of polls and campaigns.

Applications will come out of the confluence of information and other technologies. Information technology will allow for better data-gathering, analysis, planning, testing and evaluation as a basis for macroengineering. Macroengineering or planetary engineering could become one of the aspects of a continuing open-ended experiment. It could involve, for example, reversing the flow of the Siberian rivers to water the central Asian plain, or towing icebergs to the west coast of South America, or the prevention of a third big San Francisco earthquake. Earthquakes occur because stress is built up over decades as the tectonic plates slip under or past each other. When suddenly released, the stress delivers a Richter 8 to 8.3 quake if it is a big one. Richter 3 earthquakes are virtually undetectable by people. We should be able to engineer a perpetual continuous round of Richter 3's along faults to avoid that fifty- or seventy-five-year build-up cycle leading to Richter 8's.

As smart highways emerge, ultimately able to electronically take control of an automobile from ignition to destination, IT will be applied to traffic management and streets to identify the pattern of traffic at all intersections for a given distance, and orchestrate the synchrony of traffic lights to make better use of the roadway – and more importantly, better use of people's time.

The universal applications of information technology will come about in four stages; the same pattern could be said to apply to all of what we generally call information.

The first stage is data. The collection and processing of data is in good condition. Next comes the conversion of data into information. Much of the work now going on in business and government has to do with learning how to make that conversion and use that new information more effectively. The third stage, which in some areas is on the fringe of development, is converting information into knowledge. Finally, the fourth stage, where virtually nothing is being done, is wisdom.

Environmentalism will influence practically all engineering developments because of the growing global awareness that new technologies have in the past often carried with them totally unacceptable negative consequences, almost all of which could have been avoided or greatly mitigated. That historical lesson will eventually become the planning base for the future. The potential effects on the environment, long and short term, proximate and remote, will be routinely integrated into planning. The central science of environmentalism will be ecology.

Ecology itself is undergoing rapid maturation from an abstract theoretical science framed around relatively broad principles, with practical application limited to short-term research on tiny plots of land. Gathering of massive databases about whole ecosystems will be continual. There will be moves to maintain, restore or even create new ecosystems.

In the advanced nations, where an increasing percentage of time will be spent indoors, choices regarding material, design, structure and occupancy will all be influenced by the quality of indoor air, water and sound.

The policy issue central to everything about unfolding technology is the lack of positive vision. The move in this century away from the concept of progress leads to reluctance to recognise that we human beings are in control if anyone is to be in control, that the future is manageable, and that management will only come about through conscious, planned, and continuing long-term work.

In line with that policy objective, there is a real opportunity to open up to the public a broad discussion of what technology can accomplish for the benefit of each individual and society in every part of the world.

Table 1. **Likely technological accomplishments in the next decades**

- Planetary engineering, *e.g.* waste disposal into the earth's mantle
- Iceberg-towing for arid zone irrigation
- Ocean mining
- Integrated logistics, full intermodal integration–goods in transit never touched by human hands
- Intelligent vehicle highway systems
- Integrated water supply systems on a continental scale
- 120-mile-per-gallon personal vehicles
- Manufacturing for durability, reclamation, remanufacturing and recycling
- Ocean ranching/farming
- Fail-safe nuclear power plants
- Human and animal prostheses, implants and assists
- Brain technologies
- Automated farming and animal husbandry
- Outdoor robots
- Genetic diagnoses, therapies, enhancement tools
- Intelligent structures
- Dynamic structures
- Smartness in all devices, components and systems
- Weather modification
- Earthquake prevention
- Product customisation
- Simulation of all devices and systems in design
- Automated kitchen
- Full integration of ergonomics into design
- Subsurface structures
- Nanoscale products and systems
- Robotic assists for people
- Space station
- Planning for terraforming

3

FASTER, CONNECTED, SMARTER[1]

by
Hervé Gallaire
Vice-President, Xerox Corporation

1. INTRODUCTION

What compounds the difficulty in anticipating technology evolution is not just a lack of understanding of the technology *per se* – which in itself is a formidable question given the speed of change in Information Technology – but also the fact that what is possible does not always come to pass, and what comes to pass may have scarcely seemed possible. Society ultimately chooses which among all potential evolutions will become real by deciding where to invest and what to accept, adopt or reject. Sometimes it is the lack of imagination that impairs foresight, as the early history of computers vividly demonstrates: early on, no one could imagine the need for a significant number of computers, because no one could anticipate how they would be used. Sometimes it is the lack of success in creating the technological innovation that sabotages predictions – using spoken language to talk to machines is a classic example. On the other hand, while it is quite feasible today to provide video on demand, the adoption level of that technology is (as yet) simply not high enough to allow any forecasting. Meanwhile the famous paperless office is still a myth, even though all the basic ingredients do exist to make it real. And finally, even experts who have a full understanding of technical situations can get it wrong. Bob Metcalfe, the inventor of Local Area Networks in 1973, wrongly predicted in 1995 the collapse of the Internet for 1996 – what he miscalculated is the speed at which the underlying infrastructure of the Internet is being replaced to account for new requirements.

1. Eric Peters directly contributed to the MEMS section and Dan Holtshouse to the knowledge economy section. Sophie Vandebroek provided countless references to the microelectronics and MEMS sections. J.S. Brown, M. Lamming, T. Moran, M. Weiser, A. Zaenen provided, with many other colleagues, references and discussion elements.

This paper is about the future of Information Technology. No other technology has been growing as fast as IT, in either technical or business dimensions. Even if one can predict that the rate of growth is going to slow down, it will remain sufficiently fast to impact new areas of our life in ways now unforeseeable. The predictions that follow were formulated with this in mind. *Faster* in the paper's title refers to the fact that the basic evolution of semiconductors will give birth to much faster devices than those currently in use. Semiconductors will be discussed first. A particular group of microdevices, the so-called MicroElectroMechanical Systems or MEMS, will then be examined in some detail, as they will enjoy considerable expansion and exert a huge influence on our environment.

Connected and *smarter* are two complementary attributes of Information Technology. IT systems will in time exhibit much more connectedness and be capable of significantly more elaborate functions. The paper will explore, in turn: telecommunications and networking capabilities that are just around the corner; new means of communicating with computers and agent capabilities that will make systems appear smarter in their dealings with humans; and finally, business evolutions resulting from these technical capabilities. Dertouzos (1997) and Negroponte (1995) provide interesting perspectives on this evolution; see also Ichbiah (1996).

2. SEMICONDUCTORS AND ELECTRONIC INDUSTRIES

Gordon Moore, in describing the trajectory of the semiconductor and computer industry, said that "if the automobile industry had experienced the same rhythm [as the semi-conductor industry], cars would drive one million kilometers in one hour, with barely more than one fuel tank, and it would cost less to throw away your car than to pay your parking ticket". Indeed, every three years over the past thirty the semiconductor industry has been able to multiply by four the capacity of memory chips by reducing the width of a "line" inside transistors; in that same time span the power of a computer chip, measured in instructions per second (at a given cost), has doubled every year. The industry of semiconductors has grown 20 per cent per year for about 30 years. The number of transistors shipped in 1997 is staggering: ten to the seventeenth power. This number will continue to increase by 80 per cent per year, because the demand will increase. Applications will require ever more power, especially in the user interaction area (graphics, voice, language). For true language (voice) recognition, we need 1 000 MIPS at low cost, which is not yet possible. As things are made smaller, they become faster and power requirements decrease; today a 64 Megabit DRAM memory chip is as reliable as a transistor thirty years ago. A 1959 transistor sold for $6.00, which today buys a 16 Megabit DRAM. These trends apply to memory and microprocessor chips as well as communication chips. The first computer, the ENIAC, occupied 70 cubic metres; the rate of miniaturisation since then has been about an order of magnitude every ten years. The figure of merit of computers (computing power/size × cost) has improved 1 000 times every ten years. The speed of classical (CISC) architecture processors has increased 1 000 times in twenty-five years. New architectures (*e.g.* RISC) offer high performance at lower cost and lower power consumption. They move into and enable thousands of new markets and applications. Hybrid integration is another area for development, where what is sought after is not the increase in storage or computing power, but the integration of many different functions in a chip. And again, new markets are enabled (in consumer electronics, from digital cameras to phones).

Every generation of chips reduces width size by a factor of roughly 0.7, which means that the area of a chip will be roughly half that of the previous generation chip. This also means that the minimum feature is halved about every six years. A width of 0.07 microns will be reached around 2010; research aiming at 0.03 microns has begun in several parts of the world. At the same time, the thickness of the devices decreases. A thickness of about 10 molecular layers can be obtained with no loss of integrity, and layers can be piled to get even more capacity on a chip. A formidable limitation looms, however: power consumption. As more transistors are put on the chip, perhaps with decreasing capacity but with increasing frequency, the power requirements to drive the chips soar. Voltage reduction is no longer the solution. The very recent announcement by IBM regarding the use of copper for on-chip interconnect and for the top-level metal layer, replacing the current use of aluminium, is cause for optimism but not in itself sufficient. Another limitation is purely financial: the capital requirements for a factory able to produce the technology are enormous. Today, a factory producing 5 000 wafers per week using 0.25 micron technology costs over $1 billion. Its expected lifetime is five years, which means a $4 million per week depreciation. And it will cost $2 billion for a 0.18 micron technology factory.

How long can industry absorb these costs? Further reducing line width will call for X-ray technology. Natural limits of molecular layer thickness will be reached. The time-lag between development of a technology and volume production is getting longer as the technology performance improves. The 1 Gbit memory chip will take ten years to produce. Thus diversifying the use of a technology will be the key to increasing its lifetime (which otherwise is shrinking) and to amortising the huge costs of the technology R&D. Meanwhile, extrapolation from experience can continue; to some extent, relying on historical data is safe.

Obviously, the semiconductor industry is not monolithic. The phenomena described earlier apply to one of its branches, namely semiconductors used in computer systems. But the semiconductor industry benefits from general trends and progress in the electronics industry while at the same time impacting that industry through its processes.

One example of the evolution of the electronic industry has already had a tremendous impact. The size of a cellular phone[2] will ultimately be comparable with that of a wristwatch; by 2004 it will weigh under 30 grams, including the battery. (In 1984 it weighed about one kilo.) And to be sure, storage capacity, whether magnetic or optical, will continue to increase at its same steady rate. By 2004 magnetic mass data storage will reach a cost of 0.03 cents per megabyte, down from 0.25 in 1996; head tracking precision will reach 0.05 microns, from 0.2 today. In the optical storage case, the DVD (digital versatile disk) will replace the CD (compact disk) even though many people will hardly have used CDs in their computer applications; such is the speed of progress. Storage capacity will grow 15 times from today's CDs to 2004's DVDs, and read rates will increase 5 to 10 times. What will follow DVDs is unclear. To really understand the impact on how documents and books will be stored, consider the following: a new magnetoresistance technology soon to be commercialised should allow storage of up to 300 gigabytes in a PCMCIA card format (roughly $8.5 \times 5.5 \times 1$ cm); technology that could go up to 10 terabytes has been demonstrated. The latter capacity may be beyond our needs, but it will have a considerable impact on libraries and book publishing. A novel is a file of perhaps one megabyte.

Not every technology enjoys such smooth evolution. Displays technology, for example, involves many competing technologies. So much depends on the conditions of use of the display that research is necessary in several directions at once: hand-held devices, laptops, workstations, very large area displays and special displays. All these have different requirements in power, contrast ratio, resolution, brightness, viewing angle, etc. It is clear, however, that high-resolution colour flat panel displays of large dimensions will be available in the next ten years, and in many cases will be used in place of today's cathode ray tubes. These displays will be seen everywhere – replacing X-ray films, for example – and take on a key role in the medical field.

The last type of display to mention here is really not an extrapolation of what is available today. It could be called, quite simply, electric paper. Several technologies should make possible by 2005-2010 the advent of a kind of reusable paper, writeable and erasable as many times as wanted, easy to carry, and foldable to some extent. Books and folders will be made with it; it will be possible to browse through such a book and work on several pages simultaneously. Contributing technologies have been explored for more than a decade, and significant increase in performance has been achieved.

A few numbers can usefully conclude this section. The semiconductor industry worldwide is still growing at about 20 per cent per year and will top $250 bil-

---

2. *Source*: Herschel Shosteck Associates, reproduced in National Electronics Manufacturing Initiative (1996).

lion in 2000, up from $14 billion in 1982. Inside those numbers are slumps and hikes, and overproduction (especially for memory chips) is not uncommon; but the growth, it seems, can easily withstand the slumps and dramatic currency swings.

And there is no reason to believe these trends will not continue for many years to come. It is simply that we do not know how many years. When will technology depart from Moore's law?[3] Moore himself says about 2010-2015. Others also foresee this for around 2010. But it is not an all-or-nothing question. Segments of the roadmaps will continue to scale; general progress will slow down. Chip costs will continue to increase but cost/benefit per function will continue to drop. By 2010 we forecast a chip DRAM of 64 GBit, with a 0.07 micron line width and a cost of 0.2 cents per megabit, from the 256 Mbit DRAM of 1998, at a cost of 7 cents per megabit and 0.18 micron line width. Microprocessor chips will contain a staggering 60 million transistors per square centimetre and cost 0.02 millicent per transistor. Chip frequency will increase from 400 MHz today to 1 100 MHz by 2010. The storage capacity of DRAM chips will be multiplied by 4 and that of microprocessor chips will increase only by 3. The charge required will go down below 1 volt from 3.3 today. These improvement levels remain a considerable challenge. The industry is, however, extraordinarily well organised, and investing in all areas required to be successful. It will succeed.

This paper will not belabour the impact of the development of computer technology in areas where older generations of computing devices become cost-effective (and practically standard). Computers in cars are not the leading-edge microprocessors that the above figures track. They are one, two and sometimes three generations behind the state of the art. They provide at reasonable cost a nice-to-have function which sometimes becomes a vital function, replacing another technology or creating a new one. This type of impact is nonetheless extremely important for the semiconductor and electronic industries: it gives them the opportunity to amortise their developments over much longer periods, thereby generating work for many more companies and people. The "intelligent" homes, cars, etc. will all benefit from this innovation capability.

However, there will be a radical shift in the way we relate to computers. Two evolutions are resulting from microelectronics' ongoing revolution. Mark Weiser coined the term "ubiquitous computing" to describe the first one. Today's world is that of distributed computing. Ubiquitous computing will happen when all things have computers built in and these computers are connected together, so that from your car you can start preheating your oven, or your house. Being able to know the traffic situation when you go shopping, where precisely to park, etc. will

---

3. According to which, every eighteen months the capacity of microprocessors doubles.

be but one type of benefit of ubiquitous computing. The Internet is the key to make this happen, but the evolution will not come about without significant progress in the areas of wireless communications, power consumption and batteries, user interfaces and the like.

Ubiquitous computing could be in place by 2005-2010 because the infrastructure will be in place, but its development will benefit from a second evolution: what Weiser and J.S. Brown have coined "calm" technology. If computers are everywhere, it is important that they stay in our periphery; they should not be as central to our activity as today's personal computer, which requires direct and focused interaction. An analogy developed by Weiser and Brown is that of the car where the noise of the motor is in the periphery; we are sensitive to any *unusual* noise, and react immediately. A newspaper, too, carries peripheral information in its layout. Everything around us provides clues about what is important and what is peripheral. It will be some time, however, before the computer and its interactive mode achieves "calmness". 3D interaction provides a user interface that goes a step in this direction – but only a step. 2D technology with open and closed windows does not provide enough information about the periphery to qualify as a calm technology. Calling something peripheral suggests that you can easily take control of it and act upon it if required. The evolution of the Internet provides another example. While today the Internet connects computer to computer or person to person, the MBone evolution of the Internet (Multicast backBone) provides streams of traffic among multiple users and enables the flow of activities that constitute a neighborhood. What equivalent of the Web will make multicast live up to its promise and provide a notion of periphery?

Thus our environment will change radically, on the basis of the amazing success of semiconductor and electronic industries. We are continuing to ride an exponential curve in terms of semiconductor capabilities. And as cost-effectiveness and networking merge in the years to come, those changes will have an even more profound effect on our lives.

3. MICROELECTROMECHANICAL SYSTEMS (MEMS)

The semiconductor revolution consisted in being able to move electronic information from one place to another faster, more reliably and cheaper year after year. Another revolution, one similar, is under way. The information moved by microelectromechanical systems need not be electronic; it can be mechanical, chemical or biological. Two types of systems are involved, sensors and actuators. Sensors are converters of one form of energy into another; actuators allow sensors to interact with each other. MEMS uses technology from very large-scale integration to create structural components rather than transistor parts such as gates and metal contacts. Those components usually require post-processing or assembly in order to become workable devices. [See Petersen (1982) for a detailed vision of the micromachining field.]

MEMS today

Currently, commercially successful MEMS components/products are primarily found in:

1. the medical industry – silicon disposable blood pressure sensors, manufactured in the tens of millions every year;
2. the automotive industry – micromachined airbag accelerometers, also produced in the tens of millions each year; chemical sensors for emission control; air manifold pressure sensors;
3. consumer products such as inkjet printheads, projection displays and scientific instrumentation for chemical analysis systems.

Surprisingly, however, in the academic and industrial laboratories many macro-world components have found their equivalent in the micro world (feature sizes in the order of microns, overall component dimensions in the order of 100 um to few mm). Examples include micromotors, gears, transmissions, kinematic mechanisms, fluid pumps, valves, particle filters, steerable mirrors, lenses…even micromachined incandescent and internal combustion engines on a chip. This technology is not dominated by one continent or country; the state of the art is being pursued in the United States as well as in Europe and Asia.

As the field matures more and more technology pull is occurring, as opposed to the technology push of the 1980s; the emphasis is shifting to industrial R&D as well, and numerous MEMS startups are sprouting in Silicon Valley. The decade of technology/toolbox has been followed by one of commercialisation (technology as enabler of profitable applications). MEMS technology is set to become increasingly pervasive, even as it remains inconspicuous to the daily user/customer.

Application areas and the future impact of MEMS

A number of independent market studies conducted in the past five years disagree strongly on the dollar amount of future market potential (estimates range from a few billion to tens of billions), but tend to agree on the likely commercial application areas over the next five to ten years. These are: 1) mechanical and inertial devices (mostly microsensors for force, pressure, acceleration and flow, and rate gyroscopes); 2) fluidics devices (*e.g.* inkjet printheads, chemical analysis on a chip, drug screening/assays); 3) optical devices (displays, optical communication components, laser beam scanners and modulators); and 4) devices for data storage. Later still, it is very well possible that the really pervasive applications will be the ones that cannot possibly be predicted at this point; just as lasers and transistors have found their way into the home, car and PC, MEMS devices will increasingly become a part of everyday life. Extrapolations of the possible impact on Information Technology are presented below.

Potential impact on Information Technology

Information input

Optical MEMS components, such as scanning micro-mirrors or micro-lenses equipped with on-board optical detectors, will be able to acquire an image and convert it to bits; this will be done at high speed and in a package not larger than a few cubic millimetres. Low-cost human-computer interfaces based on retinal or fingerprint scanning may end up being widely used for identification purposes in virtual space transactions.

The technology to enable full inertial "navigation" on a chip is coming online. This will allow the position of an object to be tracked in space by measuring all 6 accelerations it is subject to at all points in time. The tracked object could be the gripper of a robot (which would allow robots to be much lighter for the same accuracy, which would in turn make them much faster), or a pen (an input device would transmit written data in binary form to a computer – or for identification purposes), or a glove/ring/watch for gesture-based human-machine interfaces. The technology required to implement 3 accelerometers and 3 gyros on a silicon chip is essentially available today.

MEMS-based sensors for an increasing number of physical, chemical, thermal, optical and other variables will increasingly become the eyes, ears, noses, taste buds and skin of our future information systems. Several Silicon Valley startups are investigating MEMS-based "lab-on-a-chip" concepts, *i.e.* fluid handling and (bio)chemical analysis on disposable chips that will allow a physician to perform a variety of blood tests and have the results available instantly, as opposed to sending samples to a clinical lab and having to wait hours or days.

Information output

Some of the most exciting MEMS developments are taking place in the area of information output and display.

Notably, the Texas Instruments DMD (digital mirror device), which is currently featured in high-resolution digital projectors, is a silicon chip roughly 1 centimetre^2 consisting of well over one million microscopic mirrors. Each individual mirror is electromechanically steerable, to reflect a ray of light onto the projection screen (bright pixel) or away from the screen (dark pixel). The interplay of these millions of MEMS mirrors on this chip and their on-board electronic circuits produces full-colour, full-video-rate XVGA images on a 5-foot projection screen.

On the other end of the scale, several small companies such as Microvision are working towards micro-displays, ultimately to place high-resolution colour monitor capabilities in regular style eyeglasses. One approach is to use the retina itself as the projection "screen": instead of looking at a real image projected on a monitor or screen, the virtual image ("real" and "virtual" to be understood in the optics sense) is raster scanned directly onto the retina. This can give the viewer the impression of actually looking at a 17-inch monitor 2 feet away; the viewer can decide to look at it or look away from it, focus on it or "through" it onto the physical world, or make it disappear at the flick of a switch. MEMS technology will be the key to the practicality of these novel display systems, and that practicality will be key to widespread acceptance.

Information storage

Today micromachined components can be used to replace selected compo-nents in conventional storage systems (*e.g.* hard disk drive read/write heads). There is also the potential for high-speed, high-resolution laser beam scanning systems for optical data storage. MEMS-based 3D holographic data storage and retrieval is another possibility. All of these aim at increasing the speed and/or density of data storage by many orders of magnitude; some appear to be only distant possibilities.

In any case, MEMS technology may not only allow the storage density to increase but also enable the read/write mechanisms to be reduced in size and cost, possibly to the point where these disappear into the storage media themselves.

Information processing

Several compelling applications of microfluidics can be found in the biomedical application areas. Photolithographically defined microscale fluid flow pathways, reagent reservoirs, reaction chambers and pumping mechanisms on a chip allow such applications as DNA multiplication (PCR), DNA analysis (electrophoresis on a chip), and large-scale combinatorial bio-assays that in turn allow pharmaceutical companies to use "shotgun" approaches in a cost-effective manner in drug screening tests.

Information communication

MEMS and optics are a natural combination because microscale devices can only generate microscale forces, but "no" force is needed to steer or modulate light (as opposed to MEMS micromotors or other actuators that can hardly gener-ate enough force to move their own rotor let alone drive a useful load). Many optical components have indeed already been successfully demonstrated. Several relate directly to optical communication systems, *e.g.* high bandwidth optical switches (micro-mirrors) for multiplexing in fibre-to-the-home or fibre-to-the-curb applications. Because of the fundamental scaling laws, microscale mechanical parts can operate at extremely high speeds compared to their macro-world counterparts. Megahertz operation has been demonstrated in some mechanical parts.

Indirectly, MEMS technology may have an exciting influence on future global communication systems through the work NASA, JPL and other organisations are pursuing in micro-, nano- and pico-satellites. The future trend in satellites and space ventures in general seems to be moving away from few high-cost, high-mass payloads towards many low-cost, low-mass payloads. In this context, it is possible to envision a large number of very small pico- or nano-satellites in low earth orbit serving the telecommunications needs of the future, as opposed to a handful of large satellites in geosynchronous orbit. Large numbers of these satellites could be put into orbit in a very cost-effective manner because of their low mass (tens of kilograms down to hundreds of grams) and because a low orbit suffices to span the globe if enough of them are in orbit. JPL is actively pursuing research on MEMS components to enable propulsion, control, sensing and communication systems for future generations of miniature satellites. Examples of this work include micromachined thrusters, fuel pumps, gyros, accelerometers and active cooling/heating systems. Extensive coverage of the sky with "inexpensive" satellites may eventually facilitate ubiquitous wireless network connectivity of portable or "wearable" personal information sources.

A final note on MEMS

Why have fifteen years of MEMS not had a wider impact on the world already (*i.e.* compared with the first fifteen years of microelectronics)? Is this likely to change in the future? One of the barriers is the packaging of MEMS devices, which aims at insulating them from their environment even though they need to act on their environment. Modelling tools are another barrier to some extent. Yet the use of MEMS in the printheads of inkjet printers is proof that they can be extremely successful in very competitive high-volume markets – and that in specific domains, these barriers can be overcome.

4. A NEW PARADIGM – THE NETWORK

Scott McNealy coined the phrase, "The Network is the Computer." This is profoundly true today with the advent of the Internet as a public network. But the phrase has taken on a new meaning because of the Internet's World Wide Web. The Network becomes the new interface to the computer, but also the new interface to business, to communities of people, and perhaps to the individual.

For this to become a reality – and, if it is to represent true progress – much will need to be done to develop user interface features, either over the network or apart from it. These will be described in a later section.

The same revolution that is happening with microelectronics is happening in telecommunications and networking, fuelled by microelectronic and optronic capabilities. As George Gilder puts it, "today's economy is brimming with obsolescent architectures based on scarce bandwidth, free transistors, free watts: what is changing is that bandwidth availability, technically, will outpace Moore's law that is driving the semiconductor and computer industries." This means that the fibre optics bandwidth is going to exceed any requirements we can think of today; that wireless technology itself is going to compete head-on with regular telephony, which will be under attack by Internet-based telephony; that the cable, telephone and fibre future depends on finding the proper use for the technology – not on technology limitations – and on pricing policies that deregulation cannot, in itself, bring about. It is quite likely that a combination of fibre and wireless (to the home or mobile) technology will pose a major challenge to the big operators. Every single technology is being pushed to new limits, such as copper lines that can support an 8 megabits per second bandwidth and could go to 20 Mb/s; mobile phones working a much higher frequency band could provide up to 50 gigabits per second; the fibre itself could provide these bandwidths even before we reach optical computers. Perhaps the right question to ask is, what will all that bandwidth enable? One-dial-tone capability (*i.e.* the same dial-tone used for phone, modem, fax, etc.) that can access arbitrary subscribers or data sources (video, voice) will be available around the end of the next decade.

Public switched data networks and their services will continue to expand, leading to public switched wideband (1.5 Mb/s) and broadband (50 Mb/s and up) networks. Interconnectivity with private networks will also expand, and several types of companies will capture a share of the customers; electricity utilities, for example, are becoming significant actors. However, while the unfolding of telecommunications technology and implementation of the infrastructure are key to the future of Information Technology, the impact of communications costs where distance does not matter remains to be seen. Some of the potential negative impact of this future can be seen when Internet addicts leave their lines open 24 hours a day, clogging telephony networks designed for other uses. The political implications are yet another worthwhile area to explore.

In discussing the Internet's impact on activities, it is important to bear in mind that the technical evolution – and price – of telecommunications could prove significant factors. Much has been written to date, and so only two points are discussed here: Internet communities and business.

The Internet and communities

People use the Internet for its content – what it has to offer – but also to find a community. The Internet is a market-place, as will be discussed later, but it is first and foremost becoming a set of communities – that is what has made and will continue to make it successful, whether these communities share business or non-business interests.

Communities are different from cultures; even though there is an Internet culture – one which fewer and fewer Internet users understand (where access and use are free, for example) – that culture will gradually disappear and be replaced by one more mercantile and business-oriented. More importantly, the Web and the software tools seen today will support the development of communities. There are key requirements for any system to support communities successfully; these requirements are clear, although no such system yet exists. Communities need to be technologically mediated; the technology must overcome special distance and create a sense of closeness. They must support multiple interaction styles for multiple simultaneous users; real-time interaction in particular is a much-needed characteristic. Communities require new tools like multi-user dimensions (or MUDS) to thrive. The Net will support those active rather than passive in the community. E-mail is already a first step in this direction; newsgroups are a further step. In fact there are so many concepts being developed that it is extremely difficult to guess what will emerge over time. Conversation spaces flourish, implemented in many different ways and supporting many different interaction mechanisms. MUDS and their future avatars[4] define spaces where people meet and share their interests (*e.g.* in wine, flowers, CMOS devices...) and information constantly, linking their discussions to various sorts of documents (audio, video, earlier sessions on the Web discussing related topics, etc.). They will adopt push technology to broadcast news to their members or to specific buddy lists. They will use automatic collaborative filtering to select information and advise their users.

There is an exciting future for these technologies as well on the Intranet, where corporations create new communication tools that allow crucial access to information directly from the consumer. Corporations will re-engineer their information and communication systems to benefit from these technologies. A support group, for example, will be able to share information from all over the world – without control from management – to help each other solve difficult customer problems. E-mail is not sufficient to attain these objectives. MUD-like tools will

---

4. Visual representations in Virtual Reality, at first in two and eventually in three dimensions.

be combined with 2D and 3D languages such as VRML[5] to be able to describe real-world spatial situations, as well as with audio and video data, and provide realistic descriptions of their environments. The Web's influence on business processes cannot be overemphasized – not just on commercial processes, but also on the internal processes of a company. The day will come when documentation will only be made available electronically to support sales organisation; annotations made by readers or users will be shared among all of them, enriching the concept of live documentation. Combinations of push and pull technologies will be essential to the effectiveness of these processes; profiling the participants of a community will be done routinely to ensure best use of push technology and avoid saturation and information overload. In a way, the early newsgroups supported by the Internet demonstrated that most people learn how to use their time wisely – what will be more difficult in the future will be to limit the overload from commercial communities controlling the push of information to their members. These problems will be solved satisfactorily in the next ten years for most people selecting particular communities. Teams of developers – hardware and software – working as a community will develop new processes for collaborative design that will change current notions of time-to-market in radical ways.

Agents

A key component for many of the features mentioned above is the notion of "agent". In fact, agents could be a part of almost any discussion of the Internet, because they are becoming a pervasive technology. An agent is a software programme that automates on behalf of a user or another agent a task, usually a distributed task. This is not a very novel concept, but it becomes more interesting when the agent is capable of problem-solving tasks, of developing its own objectives, of sensing its environment and acting on it, of reasoning without full knowledge of its environment, and – above all – of collaborating with other, distributed agents to resolve its task. This is where "intelligence" comes in; software approximations of "intelligent" agents will become commonplace in the near future, helped to some extent by the arrival of programming languages like JAVA which support the mobility, if not the "intelligence" *per se*, of agents. A simple form of agent was alluded to above in describing the interaction between a driver and his or her car and home appliances. Obviously the user will not want to programme all of these interactions in advance, and so agents will be used, probably in combination. It will take many years, however, before that can be done in any meaningful way. We have learned that combining objects in business applications is far from straightforward; only now are the graphical tools to make it possible

---

5. Virtual Reality markup language – like HTML (hypertext markup language), a Web browser standard.

available. Agents are much more complex in nature than objects; if the advanced applications of agents described by Negroponte or by Dertouzos take place, it will not be earlier than the end of the next decade. With Artificial Intelligence concepts involved, it is necessary to evaluate carefully what will indeed be possible on a wide scale. Technologies are currently being developed to enable an agent accessing a service to request information in a standard format; that would establish a set of common attributes to all services that deal with a particular domain, giving any agent much more applicability in that domain. The next step will be to require that services describe their (different) capabilities through common syntax. With that kind of added flexibility, agents would become truly general.

The Internet as a market-place

The Internet and the Web are bringing profound changes to business. On the one hand, new markets are emerging; on the other, there are new business models – new ways of making a profit from what is being sold. These phenomena are occurring simultaneously and will continue to develop in parallel, with a lasting impact. Consider the Web as a market-place – the numbers vary considerably according to various sources, but if is safe to predict over $200 billion per year of sales revenue in the early part of the next century. Today's most aggressive company is probably CISCO, which realises over $2 billion of sales over the Internet – and contrary to most assumptions regarding the commercial use of the Web, this is not for retail and consumer products but for expensive, complex-to-configure networking equipment. Further, it is extremely likely that the major impact of the Web will be on business-to-business, and indeed CISCO products are not bought by "users" most of the time. While EDI (electronic data interchange, between businesses) has been a relative failure, the use of the Web will be a huge success in support of business-to-business exchanges. The Web will be used to shrink distribution costs. This has a disintermediation effect. Rather than lament the impact that will have on jobs, something no one will be able to stop, we must ask ourselves what, if anything, we can re-intermediate, that consumers will be ready and willing to pay for. If it is a good analogy at all, the world of facility management services shows that it is indeed possible to create new business with a customer while cutting down the basic cost of the business that is run for this customer. Imagination will count, and although this is not the place for a full discussion of the topic, it is worrisome to see how many children in most European economies lag in computer literacy with respect to many other countries.

The Internet will, in fact, create the need for new business models. Online stores are already having an impact on standard-model businesses and provoke significant, healthy countermeasures from those businesses. The speedy development of commerce will hinge on a number of technologies that are making steady progress: user interfaces, search technologies, transactional capabilities to guarantee execution of transaction, electronic payment tools, negotiation tools, and tools to establish relations of trust between partners. Consumers will take an active role in shaping future product offerings (as well as in shaping the Web itself). Consumer communities exploiting some of the community support tools described earlier will exert considerable influence on the product designers. For the latter, in fact, this is a scary prospect. A Web-based campaign against a product or a company is hardly desirable. In terms of new business models, the big unknowns are the impact of advertising on electronic commerce and how the two will interact. The interaction between content and medium industries will become tremendously important. Radical changes, however, are not on the cards for the medium term. For example, some of today's search tools show banners that advertise specific products in the set of products that match a given query; while the price of such advertising is quite cheap today, this model is too limited and cannot last in the long run. One possibility is that bandwidth could be sponsored by content owners. Whatever the format, it is safe to predict that advertising budgets will shift slowly to the Internet.

The Internet and marketing

The Internet as a marketing tool will impact direct sales dramatically. Marketing will evolve considerably and so impact the publishing industry, the industry that supports marketing; the day will come when direct one-to-one marketing over the Net will replace – or at least reduce considerably – bulk shipping of large catalogues that have very low return on investment. Electronic catalogues will be routinely used in Internet-based procurement, which will displace and expand EDI. This will happen before consumer catalogues are substituted by electronic catalogues. The Net will also replace potential junk mailings that have a very low return on investment, because it has extremely low marginal costs. Identifying and then attracting the customer will be key in this evolution. Targeting communities will be one way to target customers.

The business of retail banking is a good illustration. It will experience profound transformations in the coming decade; most banks have not fully understood the urgency of this transformation and are leaving other financial institutions to establish leadership in the delivery of financial information. For example, Intuit, which offers financial packages, is selling its services in partnership with banks in Europe while it is selling directly and extremely successfully in the United States, posing a greater competitive threat to many banks. The partnership is creating the opportunity for selling well-targeted additional services customised for the specific customers. The trend is, however, irreversible. As always, it is better to cannibalise your own services before somebody else does it for you. The case of Encyclopaedia Britannica's loss of market share to Microsoft's CD-ROM Encarta should be food for thought. Newspaper industries are actively evaluating the Web as a distribution channel. Traditional newspapers will barely be affected until the end of the next decade – if only because no "substitution" technology (flat panel or electric paper) will be widely available before then. However, it could well be that advertising will flee to the support of electronic ads, creating a risk for newspapers and leading their cost to skyrock; they may die not because they are replaced, but because their business model cannot be sustained anymore. Coming back therefore to the future of retail banking, it may be that the real risk it runs is that customers will begin shopping over the Net for providers of services, as opposed to going to their branch. This is the deconstruction of the integrated model of a bank. There is a long way between offering electronic access to a few banking services and the disintermediation or deconstruction of the banking services, but the possible may well happen if some of the technical issues already mentioned are resolved. In particular, secure transactions will be possible shortly for many forms of electronic financial transactions. Trading over the Internet is today's reality, not tomorrow's. Certification authorities and their legal recognition are around the corner. Encryption technology and its legal implications are also becoming widely understood. It will be routinely accepted at the turn of the century that security can be guaranteed, including the perfect untraceability of the payer; many payment systems will co-exist, including electronic money, credit card or micropayment-based systems.

There are a few coming clouds for the scenarios just described that might make them collapse. These are not the technical issues referred to earlier. They are of two kinds: psychological and taxation-linked. It is not unlikely that cultural differences will stall electronic commerce, *e.g.* electronic banking; after all, even today, how much money is still dormant in French households, waiting for someone to steal it rather than being deposited in the bank? It is possible that certain cultures embrace these new technologies and ways of delivering services very slowly. Education plays a leading role here. The biggest risk, however, is the taxation of Internet transactions that is looming over the horizon despite the denials of the political world – worse, it could be that at the same time the whole Internet access business model will evolve away from the flat-fee-based structure into a (perhaps more logical) usage-based fee, where usage will be some combination of bandwidth, volume, quality of service, time, distance, etc. Too many sudden changes of this nature will surely stall the development of the electronic market-place. Huberman (1997) has developed mathematical models of the Internet where characteristic user profiles are used to access response time, congestion of networks, etc. Following his analysis, it is clear that a "free" Internet will always lead to congestion, no matter how large the pipes are. Therefore, it is safe to forecast the advent of a multi-tiered Internet, where services with certain quality levels will be paid for; they will use different, private pipes. There will be much discussion, but it will happen.

Another issue often mentioned with regard to electronic commerce and the Web in general is that of intellectual property protection, commonly described as copyright protection. The paradox is that the massive availability of information on the Web makes it less valuable for the consumer, irrespective of any value judgement on the capability of preserving intellectual property. If content is less valuable, companies or content owners will compete on more than content alone, for example on brand recognition, image, coolness and the like. This is already happening and content owners who do not realise that are in for a rude shock. For example, authors opening Websites and setting up a chat room, or doing that at their publisher's site, will become not only common but a must, just as today authors dedicate books in bookstores. Again, technology will evolve to make this simple enough to be possible for most authors. Once content is available on the Net, does it need to be protected? Can it be? Until this question is resolved it is unlikely that high value content will be distributed through the Web. A look at what happens with the electronic version of newspapers made available for pay offers a glimpse of the future. Indeed, although it is clear that the subscriber can distribute the newspaper further, the system seems to garner enough customers that it already makes business sense (The Times, WSJ, etc.). Yet there is no serious protection against copying – and why should there be if people behave rationally as they do with their paper version? However, additional services (*e.g.* search of additional information) can be expected to generate additional revenue. In essence, there is no copyright issue for the ephemeral information contained in a newspaper. But what about high value and long-lasting content? At least in the eyes of the owner it will not be made available on the Net until copying and redistribution are under control. It is true that several technologies are beginning to emerge (they will become pervasive only in the next century) that allow both for encapsulation of content in secure containers and for distribution of usage rights with the containers, thereby limiting usage of the content to what is allowed and paid for. But the fact remains that this vision of trusted viewing (publishing, printing) will take hold only when content owners believe it is secure enough. Image distribution over the Net may be the driving force here, rather than pure textual information.

Finally, it is important to discuss how the Web is going to evolve into a communication tool between people and any type of device, particularly home appliances. Although it will take many years to develop and implement, the Internet infrastructure definition has undergone a radical evolution in 1995 with the adoption by IETF, the Internet Engineering Task Force, of a new version of the basic transport mechanism involved, the so-called IP protocol. Many times rejected in favour of ISO or proprietary standards in the recent past, IP is now becoming the universal protocol and recognised as an absolute requirement. Among the features offered by the new protocol IPv6 – such as security and broadcasting capabilities – is a bewilderingly huge address space, 128 bits. This means that there will be enough addresses for virtually everyone, every computer, every appliance in the world to have its own unique address – one's toaster, phone, car, document, whatever. What this means is that every object can now become a server and provide information, data, documents (through Web pages) to any "requester", person or device. The radio can now be accessed through its electrical wire or any other Internet connection, and will tell the user, if asked, anything the user may want to know regarding its guarantee; it will also fill the user in about specific shows that it knows the user likes particularly. While it will take a decade or two for all Internet access providers, routers, etc. to make the necessary changes, the day will come. All of these features will also benefit from the development of new software technology that allows a person to download and execute locally software that normally does not reside there (because payment is required, or its lifespan is short, etc.). This is the Java concept, which, while its infrastructure is young, will probably develop much faster than the telecommunications infrastructure required to obtain full benefit from the Internet, and for that matter from IPv6 itself. Long before those are in place, the impact of Java (and other technologies) will be felt in the development of so-called thin clients, thin servers, 3-tier architectures, etc. Mainframes are not dead, but they will only be accessed by servers, not by people.

5. COMMUNICATING WITH YOUR SYSTEMS – HUMAN INTERACTION

This is perhaps the biggest unknown with regard to the future of IT. What will make the difference between a very large market accessible only to those who are computer-literate, and a huge planetary market accessible to all? It is the ease of communication between the system and the user that is going to make the difference, in a world where the cost of the basic system will decrease to very low levels, possibly zero. The PC on a chip, as mentioned, is around the corner.

Our relationship with computing devices, as well as the interaction with them to accomplish a task in a physical environment, will undergo very dramatic changes as we move to the early part of the next century. A key evolution is that of Virtual Reality, and its variants such as Augmented Reality, or wearable computers. A discussion of VR follows, along with a description of the more traditional user interface thread which offers exciting new or maturing technologies.

Virtual Reality and its variants

"Virtual environments" may be a better, more realistic way than "virtual reality" to describe the 3D interactive computer-based systems that use devices to provide a sense of presence in space to the user, be it visual, auditory or sometimes tactile or olfactive. Head-mounted, head-tracked displays, data gloves and haptic displays are examples of these devices. Virtual reality therefore allows your body, *e.g.* your head, and other objects to interact through the computer. There is a variant called Augmented Reality that differs in that it aims at using computers to enhance and augment real objects, thereby also creating a virtual environment that can be made sensitive to user's actions. An example would be a camera on a desk that enables the user to work with virtual scissors on paper, without cutting the paper, by doing cut and paste gestures with his/her fingers under the camera (or electronically). With see-through displays and projectors or hand-held displays, everyday objects can gain electronic properties. Many applications of Augmented Reality will develop in environments where the human carrying out a task will need access to information that is not available to him or her at the time. For example, using head-mounted displays, the service engineer will see and read the pages of the manual that are needed to repair what their hands are currently trying to fix. Prototypes exist, and technical difficulties with the interfaces are being solved. It will be possible to see inside a car or a printer using a finger, and navigate by turning the head or talking to the computer.

Calm computing was mentioned earlier as a possible evolution of computing. Wearable computers are becoming a reality, the obvious precursors of calm computing technology. A watch can behave as a computer, exchanging information with a PC and delivering today's schedule or e-mail without any wire attachment and with a very crude interface. In the next century, clothes will integrate computer chips and react to the environment, the temperature, even other people. Component technology described earlier such as MEMS will enable tools such as spatial trackers, which are important for making more acceptable head-mounted displays, in particular glasses and gloves. Eye-tracking systems are also making good progress, but lag behind gloves and finger movement tracking; this technology already has been demonstrated to be capable of, for example, allowing a person to play music by tapping on their desk. Displays can be also be used to provide a sense of spatial presence – either video displays (teleconferencing) or wall-size displays (media spaces). None is as effective as Virtual Reality or Augmented Reality. Teleconferencing success will continue but its role will not expand significantly; it will not provide the sense of community or physical presence that is truly required. In media-space environments, spatial gesture recognition is the ingredient that is necessary to create Augmented Reality. Interacting with a display and using a tool that can capture and react to gestures is a very attractive environment for discussion or design meetings. The technology exists and is maturing. It may, however, be replaced by the use of cameras and image analysis tools that will also allow actions in response to gestures. Workgroup discussions and lectures will take quite a different turn when gestures are interpreted and executed in the electronic virtual world but act on the real world. Gesture languages will be developed and perhaps even specialised for specific domains. In practice, what will be used will be a combination of gesture recognition and audio or video capture, in order to be able to annotate meetings. The user interaction with the wall display, electronic or not, will allow fluidity of actions – and display awareness will be reduced so that it remains in the background, in the periphery. This will help to avoid inhibiting participants in the meeting who may otherwise feel accountable for their statements beyond what occurs in a typical meeting. What is possible on these large interactive displays will also be possible in other environments where computers and other devices will vie to provide a virtual and augmented world at the same time. Design and problem-solving meetings will become documents that can be used more effectively than was previously possible.

The personal document reader is another device that will provide a virtual environment in which paper is emulated. PDRs will require significant progress in displays because they will have to be light and sturdy, with good reflecting or emitting characteristics, etc. The electric paper technology described earlier is a candidate technology, although flat-panel-based PDRs will exist before electric paper does. The PDR will reproduce the way paper is manipulated; it needs to display at least two pages at a time, provide capabilities to browse text, place markers, annotate, etc. This will be a virtual rendering of the real tool, paper. But as with other virtual and augmented environments, much benefit can be obtained by being in an electronic environment that adds dimensions to the "paper" environment; if you stumble on a word you may immediately access a dictionary; you may link to a Website to look for additional information. The set of possibilities is infinite. Does this mean that because most or nearly all source documents will be (if they are not already) in electronic form, we will not need paper and will have reached the famed state of paperless office? The answer is no; in fact, all indications are that paper usage will grow at least for the next ten years. PDRs will be used in niches. Paper has many "affordances" that will always be difficult to reproduce – not just its physical qualities, which are obvious, but also the way it is used, the way the human eye can read; paper reading is indeed still more efficient – and enjoyable – than screen reading – and will be for a long time. Just as importantly, PDRs will not display the same information as paper if they are to be successful. A newspaper displayed on a PDR will probably be presented in a different way from the conventional newspaper, to differentiate itself and attract readers.

Personalised display and reading and personalised contents will be the norm for these PDRs, using the agent technology described earlier.

In summary, in parallel to the development of cheap and powerful devices – computers or MEMS, cameras or sensors of all sorts – our relation to the environment is going to change significantly. In particular, not all the implications of the digital camera and its capabilities – soon to be integrated into your computing environment at reasonable cost – are as yet understood.

User interface (UI)

Even if none of the above becomes mainstream, the interface to the computer as we know it today will undergo significant evolutions, led by the technological evolution and by the need to support professionals or people not sufficiently computer-literate. The major trend is towards multi-modality and multiple media. Using multiple modalities to communicate with the computer, simultaneously or not, will bring real improvements to most tasks. Modalities that are not used today will become commonplace; others will evolve at different paces. Voice recognition will be the single biggest growth segment in the user interface domain. A version where the speaker does not need to pause between words will be available before 2010. Multilocutor speech with simultaneous speakers will not be cracked by that time. The range of applications open is very wide indeed even in monolocutor connected speech. Note-takers will be commonplace; database or Web querying will be routinely available, as will order-giving tools. Specialised PDAs will appear initially. For limited knowledge domains some of these applications, where the computer is trained in specific technical domains, are already available. Domain independence is a much harder issue. Beyond speech recognition, speech understanding will continue to prove elusive in all likelihood although true dialogue with a system will be possible in well-defined contexts (document search, for example). In this category, handwriting recognition will make significant inroads but will not become mainstream when it is unconstrained; there is more variability in writing than in speech. Languages for a simplified handwriting will become more widespread, able to take abbreviations into full account, but voice will replace most of their uses as time goes by.

Natural language understanding is the complement of speech understanding. Many people equate natural language technology and translation technology. This need not be, and indeed much has been done that does not require the true natural language understanding capability that enables full translation: morphological analysis and syntactic analysis are pretty much understood and embedded into products such as text editors, search tools or grammar checkers; progress will continue to be made in these applications, providing a much broader range of features and of languages at reduced cost. Syntax checkers and grammar checkers are less advanced than their morphological counterparts; however, with the introduction of large semantic databases that link related concepts the performance of these grammar checkers will near 100 per cent and will be above most people's capabilities. (Even a perfect system won't remove the ambiguity of "I saw the man with a telescope".) Technical documents, for example, will easily be analysed and checked, provided the technical domain will have been described. These tools then open the door to translation technology. Today's so-called automatic translation is not doing what it advertises. It is at best a help to translation – working better, as always, when it is limited to technical contents. Machine translation will continue to be "aided" – more powerful tools will be at work, providing support to report authors and translators in unprecedented ways; the use of translation memory will become pervasive; the translation system will elicit answers from humans to remove the few ambiguities that it cannot resolve. While the translating telephone, where people at each end speak a different language, will not be available any time soon, speech and language understanding combined will allow direct interactions with systems. Natural language applications to content management (search, retrieval, indexing, summarising) will make great strides, in particular summarising. Automatic summarising is available today; what will be developed further is the possibility to annotate your document to provide genre definition, hints to the summariser and the like. Natural language and speech are the big winners of the next decade on the UI side.

Keyboard and display will remain very much present in our environment. Not that they will not undergo significant changes: keyboard and mouse will evolve to allow input with two hands in design activities – this is a non-trivial technology evolution that will also produce many innovations to replace the mouse or allow its acceleration, even on PCs; the ability to combine the cursor (the mouse) with more elaborate functions than the mouse clicks (even the menus available by mouse clicking) will provide greater productivity. The concept of ToolGlass has been developed to greatly enrich the interaction, providing a kind of mobile palette attached to the cursor but transparent so that the underlying design can still be seen. Display evolution has already been mentioned; personal digital assistants, PDAs, will continue to be used with much-improved UIs, especially Web-based. Mobile phones linked to the Internet, for example, will have much better display capability and voice input to make them a challenging alternative to many uses of laptops – especially given that infrared links to other devices will allow them easy communication with a host of services yet to be created.

Another area for significant change is the area of data visualisation or, more generally, information visualisation, and even spatial visualisation. What emerges from current research will tie in with other efforts like 3D viewing tools, the Web, ubiquitous computing and the like. One of the well known limitations of the current Windows-based user interfaces is that they can only represent several dozen objects at any given time, and these objects have no situational relationship to each other. The metaphor is called desktop, yet it is a very poor imitation of real desktops; for applications that are not intended to describe a desk, it does not do much. We need new widgets to view and manipulate information based on an underlying structure yet to be invented. Such widgets could include: perspective walls, document pages, hierarchy representation tools, tabular representation tools, special calendars and time representation tools. These and other tools must be developed to support both focus and context. This is the key to the notion of calmness developed earlier. We need to provide perception representation, through graphical means, of the object (numbers, etc.) being manipulated. We need to provide animated transitions that support tracking changes – what cognitive psychology has been advocating for a long time. A few examples of current lab technologies are given below, where the cognitive and the perceived reinforce each other. A set of numbers, when there are many numbers, does not tell us very much. The same set when represented in a way that exhibits irregularities and salient features immediately takes on another dimension. In a spreadsheet where monthly results are represented branch by branch and product by product, if numbers are replaced by coloured segments linked with certain thresholds, 1 000 lines can be represented at once, and if there are patterns they leap to the eyes. A "cone tree" can be a technique to represent extremely large hierarchies like a file system topology or a network topology: understanding, perception and navigation can be helped tremendously by such a tool, which does allow focus and context; combined with colours it allows a network to be surveyed very effectively; combined with 3D motion it gives superfast access to the right location, showing its context. There will be other tools that will build on these concepts, and relieve the user from being overloaded with useless information. Yet another tool, expanding the desktop metaphor, proposes a 3D view of the office, the desk, shelves, etc. – presenting pages as pages, books as books, shelves as shelves, showing our office objects in perspective as we see them, allowing for their direct manipulation, creating for example books from (Web) pages to put on shelves for further reference. We have here a much more powerful concept that begins to provide context and forms to the user of the "office". Deep intuition is necessary to create these new forms of interfaces, but this is not enough. It is absolutely necessary to call upon the expertise of social sciences which bring to the fore such notions as the importance of context.

This large number of concepts to describe the future of UIs and also of our environments indicate a thriving and promising field. UIs will receive yet another boost with the use of paper as an interactive object thanks to the swift development of digital cameras, digital pens, wireless communications, etc.

6.   TOWARDS A KNOWLEDGE ECONOMY

We may still speak of Information Technology, but we are definitely dealing with concepts other than information. Data and knowledge are also manipulated by computers. A continuum exists between these three concepts. There is undoubtedly a new emphasis on knowledge and its management. While it may be presented as the latest fad driven by consultants, book publishers and conference organisers, it does correspond to a deeper and pervasive movement that even affects the economy; we are going from a manufacturing and services economy to a knowledge economy. Although knowledge about competition, customers, markets, technologies, processes, communities, etc. has always been critical to business success, the importance of knowledge and one's knowledge assets in today's firm is such that there is a ground swell for a much more explicit and systematic way to manage them in a firm. For example, intellectual property is becoming a key tool of the firm. IBM generates $1 billion per year on licensing alone. The knowledge obsolescence rate is accelerating, and therefore the need to store, communicate and share knowledge is increasing rapidly. Tools such as the Internet and the Web further make this possible and boost the acceleration factor, with organisational implications for middle managers. With the pressure on knowledge work productivity mounting, adding resources to work is not the path to growth; knowledge tools are required, but so is a good understanding of the cultural aspects of the workplace and interworkings of "communities of practice". Translating these general ideas into tools and behaviours will occupy IT management and research for the next decade.

An example of a community sharing model is that of a social/technical infrastructure developed for technicians to share and build their service repair knowledge. While this does not replace formal training, it has an obvious implication for customer service, and therefore on the bottom line of the company. The incentive to contribute is not, interestingly enough, financial; it is personal recognition. Understanding what can be endorsed is as important as the technology itself.

Something therefore needs to be done to support knowledge work, above and beyond what is already done, in a more systematic manner. Tools need to be developed to foster the continuous creation, aggregation, and use/reuse of both organisational and personal knowledge; these three processes are highly interdependent processes and therefore the tools will need to be integrated. Knowledge in this context is about expertise and skills of the firm, business processes that support knowledge work, explicit knowledge repositories, and intellectual property. Therefore knowledge management systems will require the development of repositories and libraries, tools to support knowledge navigation, mapping and simulation, and tools to ease the flow of knowledge. Just to take an example, databases are not appropriate to support knowledge work. It is not acceptable to go through an administrator in order to create knowledge bases. Navigation will be supported by new visualisation, summarisation, indexing, search tools. For example, extracting topics from news wires to support intelligence work will need new tools. Automatic classification of genres of documents will help the knowledge worker. Importantly, these tools will be customisable by the knowledge worker, to match his or her own interests. Push and pull technologies will support the flow of knowledge, with negotiation tools in the middle. Knowledge flow mechanisms will be built to anticipate, suggest, elaborate on, steer and initiate connections between knowledge workers and sources of needed knowledge.

To close, two aspects of knowledge management need to be emphasized. It differs from Information Technology, which has been used mainly to rationalise, optimise and cut costs, in that it aims at improving productivity of the knowledge workers, not at replacing them. Second, it will probably follow a path similar to IT. We have seen specialised systems develop first, supporting certain areas of the business; only recently do we begin to see enterprise-wide systems that link the specialised systems. The same pattern will apply to knowledge management. We need customer support, sales support, best practices support, support systems and much more. At the same time, only when systems are integrated and information or knowledge is shared between them can we reap the true benefits of the approach; this is not for tomorrow.

7. BUSINESS PERSPECTIVES

As IT evolves to create a connected world, connecting people to community, devices to devices, people to devices; as IT gives birth to knowledge technology; as interfaces and relationships to our systems evolve, so will the IT-based economy. This last section examines some of the consequences that connectedness and *its* consequence, globalisation, are going to have on the IT economy, and on the economy in general.

A major part of the economy is dependent on IT. One cannot overemphasize the role of "the network", beyond its technical consequences; as we have discussed, networks and computers or systems or devices are really what are talked about. What if communications and hardware really become commodities? In this economy, more generates more, contrary to what is happening in the manufacturing economy – that more people are on AOL gives more value, not less, to AOL; fax has value only if more people are connected; and the same holds for e-mail, the Web, and so on. Because of this behaviour, success and return become governed by the "winner takes all" paradigm. When success shows up, it is big. The key to surviving, and therefore leading, in this economy is therefore to anticipate the time where there will be enough faxes and enough subscribers to enjoy a major success. Xerox pulled out of the fax business that it created because there was no infrastructure – not enough faxes; cost of re-entry was very high. The snowball effect is what explains the "winner takes all" and AOL overtaking Compuserve. Anticipation of the point at which the market takes up is crucial. In this economy, everything gets cheaper, and that factor needs to be accounted for in business plans since more generates more. In this economy, the faster you move and create new products, the better, and you must cannibalise your own products or someone else will do it for you. This is an economy of growth, not an economy of optimisation. Which really takes us back to the knowledge economy versus the IT economy; and who said knowledge is all about networking, *i.e.* relationships? In summary, it will be a very different economy indeed.

BIBLIOGRAPHY

ALLAIRE, P. (1997), "Managing for Knowledge: The Business Imperative of the 21st Century", *Knowledge in International Corporations*, Carnegie Bosch Institute and Carnegie Mellon University, pp. 6-8.

ANDERSON, C. (1995), "The Internet – The Accidental Superhighway", *The Economist,* 1 July.

ASOKAN, A., P.A. JANSON, M. STEINER and M. WAIDNER (1997), "The State of the Art in Electronic Payment Systems", *IEEE Computer*, September, pp. 28-35.

BASS, L. *et al.* (1997), "The Design of a Wearable Computer", *CHI 97,* ACM, pp. 139-146.

BAUDEL, T. and M. BEAUDOUIN-LAFON (1993), "Charade: Remote Control of Objects Using Free-hand Gestures", *Communications of the ACM,* 36(7), pp. 28-35.

BELL, G. and J.N. GRAY (1997), "The Revolution Yet To Happen" in P.J. Denning and R.M. Metcalfe (eds.), *Beyond Calculation*, Springer-Verlag.

BERLIN, A.W. and K. GABRIEL (1997), "Distributed MEMS: New Challenges for Computation", *IEEE Computational Science & Engineering*, January-March, pp. 12-16.

BIER, E., M.C. STONE, K. FISHKIN, W. BUXTON and T. BAUDEL (1994), "A Taxonomy of See-through Tools", *CHI 94,* ACM, pp. 517-523.

BOLLIER, D. and C.M. FIRESTONE (1996), *The Future of Electronic Commerce,* The Aspen Institute.

BROWN, J.S. and P. DUGUID (1995), "The Social Life of Documents", *Release 1.0,* October, pp. 1-18.

BRYZEK, J., K. PETERSEN and W. McCULLY (1994), "Micromachines on the March", *IEEE Spectrum,* May, pp. 20-31.

CAIRNCROSS, F. (1995), "Telecommunications, the Death of Distance", *The Economist,* 30 September, pp. 5-28.

CARD, S.K., G.G. ROBERTSON and W. YORK (1996), "The WebBook and the Web Forager: An Information Workspace for the World Wide Web", *CHI 96,* ACM, pp. 111-117.

DERTOUZOS, M. (1997), *What Will Be*, HarperEdge.

DYSON, E. (1997), *Release 2.0: A Design for Living in the Digital Age*, Broadway Books, Chapter 2 ("Communities"), pp. 31-54.

EVANS, P.B. and T. WIRSTER (1997), "Strategy and the New Economics of Information", *Harvard Business Review,* September-October, pp. 71-82.

FERBER, J. (1995), *Les Systèmes Multi-Agents*, Inter Éditions.

FUKUMOTO, M. and Y. TONOMURA (1997), "Body Coupled FingerRing: Wireless Wearable Keyboard", *CHI 97*, ACM, pp. 147-154.

GILDER, G. (1996), "The Gilder Paradigm", *Wired*, December, pp. 127-128.

GROSS, N. (1997), "Into the Wild Frontier", *Business Week*, 23 June, pp. 72-84.

HELDMAN, R.K. (1993), *Future Telecommunications, Information Applications, Services & Infrastructure*, McGraw-Hill, New York.

HINDEN, R.M. (1996), "IP Next Generation – Overview", *Communications of the ACM*, 39 (6), pp. 61-71.

HUBERMAN, B. (1997), "Storms Brewing on the Internet Horizon", *PC Week*, 13 October, pp. 98-100.

ICHBIAH, D. (1996), *L'empire invisible*, Éditions Village Mondial.

INSTITUTE FOR INFORMATION STUDIES (1996), *The Emerging World of Wireless Communications*, IIS.

INSTITUTE FOR INFORMATION STUDIES (1997), *The Internet as Paradigm*, IIS.

JACOBSON, J., C. TURNER, J. ALBERT and P. TSAO (1997), "The Last Book", *IBM Systems Journal*, 36 (3).

JUDGE, PAUL C. (1997), "Care to Slip into Something More Digital?", *Business Week*, 20 October, p. 60.

KELLY, K. (1997), "New Rules for the New Economy", *Wired*, September, pp. 140-196.

MacINTYRE, B. and S. FEINER (1996), "Future Multimedia User Interfaces", *Multimedia Systems*, 4, pp. 250-268.

MAKIMOTO, T. (1997), "Market and Technology Outlook in the Year 2000", *IEEE*.

McINTOSH, S. (1997), "Conquering Semiconductor's Economic Challenge by Increasing Capital Efficiency", *IEEE*.

MICHALSKI, J. (1995), "What's a Zine", *Release 1.0*, 23 June.

NATIONAL ELECTRONICS MANUFACTURING INITIATIVE (1996), *National Electronics Manufacturing Technology Roadmaps*.

NEGROPONTE, N. (1995), *Being Digital*, Alfred A. Knopf, New York.

O'DAY, V.L., D.G. BOBROW and M. SHIVELEY (1996), "The Social-Technical Design Circle", Proceedings of ACM Computer Support of Collaborative Work, ACM Press.

OFTA [Observatoire Français des Techniques Avancées] (1996), *Nouvelles Interfaces Hommes-Machine*, OFTA.

O'HARA, K. and A. SELLEN (1997), "A Comparison of Reading Paper and On-line Documents", *CHI 97*, ACM, pp. 335-342.

PEDERSEN, E.R., K. McCALL, T. MORAN and F. HALASZ (1993), "Tivoli: An Electronic Whiteboard for Informal Work Group Meetings", *INTERCHI 93*, pp. 509-516.

PETERS, E. (1996), "Large-Market Applications of MEMS", National Academy of Engineering Symposium on Frontiers of Engineering, National Academy Press.

PETERSEN, K. (1982), "Silicon as a Mechanical Material", *Proceedings of the IEEE,* 70 (5), pp. 420-457.

POTTENGER, M., B. EYRE, E. KRUGLICK and G. LIN (1997), "MEMS: The Maturing of a New Technology", *Solid State Technology,* September, pp. 89-98.

RAO, R. (1996), "Quand l'information parle à nos yeux", *La Recherche,* 285, pp. 66-73.

SEMICONDUCTOR INDUSTRY ASSOCIATION (1997), *The National Technology Roadmap for Semiconductors.*

TAPSCOTT, D. (1995), *Digital Economy: Promise and Peril in the Age of Networked Intelligence,* McGraw-Hill, New York.

TOKORO, M. (1993), "The Society of Objects", SONY CSL Technical Report, Addendum to the OOPSLA'93 Conference Proceedings.

WEISER, M. and J.S. BROWN (1997), "The Coming Age of Calm Technology" in P.J. Deming and R.M. Metcalfe (eds.), *Beyond Calculation,* Springer-Verlag.

4

BIOTECHNOLOGY FOR THE 21st CENTURY

by

Werner Arber

Biozentrum der Universität Basel, Switzerland

Mathis Brauchbar

Locher, Brauchbar & Partner AG, Basel, Switzerland

At the turn of the 21st century biotechnology (including gene technology) is seen as the key technology for the future. It is not a new science, but comprises a series of strategies and methods for the study and use of the genetic make-up of organisms and the relevant biological functions. It provides basic scientific knowledge on vital processes. Such knowledge may lead to applications that are to the benefit of mankind. Since modern biotechnology goes back only a few decades, its possibilities are by no means exhausted, although it is difficult to assess their range and impact. Modern biotechnology is therefore a scientific and technical development trend which is at the beginning of its technological and economic life cycle. Early on, scientists turned their attention to possible risks in gene technology. With the increasing knowledge of the mechanisms of vital functions, it is possible to have a clearer idea of these risks.

INTRODUCTION

The earth started to exist as part of the solar system about 4.5 billion years ago, and simple forms of life probably developed for the first time 3.5 to 4 billion years ago. In the course of biological evolution astonishingly varied forms of life emerged – from micro-organisms to highly developed plants and animals, all of which have different kinds of capabilities. Man is one of some 10 million different species. He is no doubt the only one to have acquired the ability to think about the essence and mechanisms of life and to benefit from the knowledge acquired. The development and use of science and technology by man is part of his cultural evolution.

Biotechnology, including gene technology,* also came into being in the course of this process, making it possible to study vital functions at molecular level and to use this knowledge for economic purposes. Biotechnology is concerned with a central aspect of life: the genetic records of a cell. Information which is necessary for the survival and the multiplication of a cell can be modified. Theoretically the cells of all organisms can be genetically modified, whether we are speaking of algae, mice, bacteria or maize plants.

Various organisms play a part in greatly different spheres of human life, and are the subject of scientific research. Many antibiotics are produced from microorganisms. Beer is brewed with yeast and dough rises with yeast. Plants are used as basic foodstuffs and also as feed for many animals which provide us with meat, milk and eggs. Wherever forms of life exist or provide services for mankind, modern biotechnology and, accordingly, gene technology also have their place. Biotechnology and gene technology thus concern different spheres of life, and consequently quite different value concepts.

Gene technology is now mainly used in medicine and in biological and biomedical research. But the processes and products concerned have also gained a foothold in recent years in agriculture and in food processing. A high proportion of the enzymes in washing powders are genetically produced. Gene technology is also used in biological warfare research. Genetic applications in the environment field, the regeneration of raw materials, cosmetics and a number of other sectors will probably be seen in the next few years.

It is, however, difficult to take stock and look ahead with any certainty, since:

- In many cases, the future technical and economic relevance of basic research in biotechnology (and gene technology) can only be guessed at.

- So far, no clear distinction has been made in statistics between traditional biotechnology (*e.g.* beer brewing) and modern biotechnology (production of recombinant drugs), on either the R&D or the production sides.

---

* **Biotechnology** refers to the technical use of organisms or their component parts (cells, proteins, nucleic acids or carbohydrates). It is therefore a blanket concept.
Traditional biotechnology mainly uses naturally occurring organisms and parts of them (*e.g.* to make beer, bread, cheese and drugs).
Modern biotechnology expands that definition to include genetics-based and other molecular biology methods (*e.g.* hybridoma technology for the production of monoclonal antibodies).
Gene technology is the sum of all methods for the isolation, characterisation and selective modification and transfer of a genetic make-up. Gene technology at present has practical applications mainly in the biotechnology and medical fields. But in the past twenty years it has also become an indispensable strategy in research on the molecular mechanisms of vital functions. Gene technology is therefore used in fundamental research as well as in commercial biotechnology.

- It is also difficult to identify the economic dividing line between biotechnology and gene technology: as cross-sectional technologies, they cannot be assigned to a particular field of industrial application, as they are involved in innovation within a whole series of existing or newly emerging sectors (especially in the chemical and pharmaceutical industries, but also in the food, beverages and tobacco industries or the developing environmental industry).

- Economic analyses and estimates of potential are usually based on very rough and theoretically unsatisfactory dividing lines between traditional and modern biotechnology (including gene technology).

In addition, the economic application of modern biotechnology has just started, which makes it difficult to produce extrapolations and trend analyses since the database is still very limited and lacking in homogeneity, and therefore also questionable.

The following pages therefore examine the origins and methods of modern biotechnology before discussing biotechnology and gene technology applications and their possible future development. The risk and safety debate has played a prominent role in the development to date of biotechnology. These aspects will therefore also be addressed.

CLASSICAL AND MOLECULAR GENETICS

Genetics began somewhat more than a hundred years ago and was based on the following observations: individual organisms which belong to the same species have by and large the same characteristics, but they may differ from one another as far as certain details are concerned. A dog, for example, is always a dog, but there are obviously different breeds because their outward appearances (phenotypes) differ. If the same characteristic is found in parents and their progeny, the latter have inherited it. Classical genetics deals with the natural laws that govern this heredity.

Chromosomes were identified as the carriers of inheritance information. In higher forms of life, these chromosomes are packed in the cell nucleus. Research in classical genetics is firstly concerned with individual organisms that differ from the standard and exhibit a transmissible outward form, such as flowers with abnormal colours. Such variants are attributed to changes in the inheritance information (mutations). By crossing independent mutants, geneticists can determine the part of a chromosome on which the change is located. Such experiments are used to produce so-called gene maps showing on which part of a chromosome a characteristic, or a gene responsible for this characteristic, is located. This does not reveal anything, however, about the chemical nature of the transmission.

This puzzle was solved about fifty years ago: it was proved through experiments with bacteria that a so-called nucleic acid is the inheritance information carrier in chromosomes. It is now known by the abbreviation DNA. Shortly afterwards Francis Crick and James Watson also described the structure of DNA as an extremely long and very thin thread molecule. Owing to its appearance, DNA was also described as a double helix. A gene, *i.e.* an inherited characteristic, corresponds to a short segment of the long genetic constitution thread. The discovery of the chemical nature of genetic make-up was followed by the development of molecular genetics, or the study of genes and their activities.

INHERITANCE INFORMATION AND ITS IMPACT

Inheritance molecules as such still do not constitute life. For life to exist the inheritance information in DNA must be read and translated into other "languages". A DNA molecule can have effect only when its genetic information is transferred to other biological molecules, which are usually proteins. Proteins serve so to speak as intermediaries between the inheritance information stored in the chromosomes and the signs of life in an organism. In the 1950s and 1960s researchers were able to explain how this intermediary function works at cell level. It transpired that these translation processes were identical for all forms of life. The "language" of inheritance is universal, meaning that it is spoken by all organisms.

The genetic make-up of a bacterium cell contains from several hundred to a few thousand genes, depending on the type of bacterium. However, not all genes have to be simultaneously active in order to maintain life in a bacterium. On the contrary, every gene must go into action at the right time. The situation is similar but still more complex with higher forms of life. For example, human beings have between 50 000 and 100 000 different genes that are important to life. However, not all of them are active in every cell and produce the appropriate proteins. This is also quite logical, for the digestion enzyme has it rightful place in the intestines and not in the brain. On the other hand, it would not be very logical if liver cells produced antibodies. Accordingly, every type of cell activates the particular range of genes whose activity it requires, while the other genes remain inactive and at rest.

It should be remembered that each of the cells in the body of an adult human being – and these number something like 5×10^{13} – is equipped with the full range of human hereditary information, the human genome. Owing to this complexity, the body clearly has to control gene activity very accurately. Particular genes are usually switched on and off by specific substances which control their activity. These control substances are again frequently produced by genes.

But how can all these biological functions be investigated and assigned to the corresponding hereditary information? In the last thirty years a whole series of research strategies and methods have been developed for this purpose. Gene technology is of central importance in this respect.

Viruses and very small bacterial chromosomes, or plasmids as they are called, can serve as natural gene vehicles. Microbial geneticists had already observed in the 1950s that the genetic make-ups of certain viruses and bacteria can intermix when these viruses attack bacteria in order to multiply. When this happens, the viral genetic make-up can absorb parts of the bacterial genetic make-up. The virus then serves as a vehicle which transfers the bacterial gene from one host cell to another. The hereditary information transferred to other bacteria can thereby be expressed, and accordingly give the receiving cell characteristics which it previously did not possess. At the time researchers were amazed by this intermix of hereditary information from quite different sources, but the phenomenon has since been confirmed a great many times.

RECOMBINATION OF HEREDITARY MATERIAL *IN VITRO*

Around 1970 American researchers succeeded for the first time in recombining *in vitro* a piece of known gene information with the genetic make-up of a virus. The DNA incorporated into the virus subsequently multiplied in the host bacteria, and the transmitted gene information was expressed.

In the 1970s molecular biologists developed chemical methods that made it possible to read accurately the alphabet (sequence) of DNA fragments over a few hundred components. They thus succeeded in deciphering genetic script. Since then the technique for this sequence analysis has been continuously improved. Nowadays the process is frequently mechanical. It has therefore become possible to decipher the entire genetic make-up of an organism: today the full sequence of hereditary information is known for a series of different types of bacteria as well as for bakers' yeast. International co-operation in this field is extremely active, and it can be foreseen that in the next decade or two the hereditary information sequence of human beings, as well as that of many other organisms, will be fully identified.

A great deal of work, however, remains to be done. This can be illustrated by considering the size of genomes, in which the number of DNA components can be compared with the number of letters in books and libraries. An intestinal bacterium has a genetic endowment of some 4.7 million components – roughly the number of letters in a thick book the size of the Bible. A gene, or hereditary characteristic, would correspond from a few lines to two pages in this book. In comparison, the diploid, human genetic material with its 46 chromosomes and some 6 000 million components, would be the equivalent of a library containing about 1 500 books.

In the case of *in vitro* recombination and the production of genetically modified organisms, usually a single gene or a few genes are transplanted, which is equivalent to adding from one to a few pages to the receiving organism's library. The organism therefore keeps most of its characteristics. So far all genes transplanted *in vitro* have been natural genes. Artificial active genes with new types of capabilities have not been produced so far.

GENE FUNCTIONS

When a molecular geneticist has identified the DNA sequence in an organism's genetic make-up, his work is by no means over; it has just started. His aim is to understand the mechanisms of vital functions. But the sequence of hereditary information components gives no direct information on its mechanism. Conclusions about the function of a DNA sequence can only be drawn if an almost identical sequence in another organism has already been identified as the information for a specific biological characteristic. Such conclusions about the function can be drawn from the sequence by comparing DNA data banks.

The gene's hereditary information often has to be slightly modified if the gene's function is to be studied. This deliberately modified gene is incorporated in living cells or organisms so that its impact can be examined. While classical geneticists keep an eye on randomly occurring mutations, molecular geneticists make highly selective changes to the genetic endowment. They can accordingly take a much more systematic approach.

If an inherited characteristic of an animal or plant is being investigated, the modified gene can be used either for cells obtained from cultures or for complete organisms. In the second case, the genetic modification is frequently made to the organism's germline. In many (but not all) cases the gene technology modification of cells and the germline has the same result. The results obtained with whole organisms are usually considered more relevant than those obtained with cell cultures. For this reason it is often essential to work with so-called transgenic organisms, if reliable results are to be produced from the investigation of genetic functions.

For ethical reasons, however, there is a universal consensus that genetic modifications to human germ cells cannot be permitted. In several countries genetic modifications to the human germline are prohibited. Such modifications are also prohibited by the Council of Europe's Bioethics Convention. Already for purely scientific and technical reasons, it would hardly occur to any researcher to investigate human genetic functions by means of a genetic change to the germline. For as a rule a few generations of transgenic organisms are needed to explain biological functions. Accordingly, an experiment on a human being would take several decades. Experiments with conventional laboratory animals such as mice are a good substitute for experimentation on human beings.

It may be appropriate to make a short statement at this point. Gene technology comprises a series of usually very selective and informative research strategies and methods, too many to be discussed in this report. They mostly involve a selective and often localised intervention in the genetic material of an organism. In that respect there is a marked difference between gene technology and classical genetics. Although work on mutants is also carried out in the latter field, the modifications to the genetic make-up are not so selective. According to our definition, artificial insemination *in vitro* and the transfer of embryos to the womb do not come under gene technology since they leave the genetic endowment concerned quite intact. Conventional plant and animal breeding has just as little to do with gene technology.

BENEFITS OF NEW FINDINGS

Since about 1980 the industrial world has been increasingly interested in the use of basic research findings in the molecular genetics field. This has given biotechnology a real, new boost. Genetically produced drugs and products for medical diagnoses have become available relatively quickly, such as interferon for the treatment of certain types of cancer and for reliable AIDS tests. The impetus of this universal trend relies to a large extent on new knowledge of biological processes. Research programmes for the development of new practical applications may contribute in the short term to more rapid progress, but in the long term new applications will greatly depend on the findings made available by basic research.

The use of biotechnology and gene technology in medicine represents a kind of quantum leap. On the one hand, gene technology gives a deeper, molecular insight into bodily functions and opens up new possibilities for diagnosis, prevention, prognosis and treatment. This includes, for example, diagnosis at the molecular genetics level or gene therapy. On the other hand, new drugs and novel types of drugs can be genetically produced. Modern biotechnology therefore supports the trend towards promoting health through preventive and prognostic measures and not just therapeutically.

So far modern biotechnology has had the greatest impact on the development and production of new medicines and new diagnostics, and on vaccines. In all these fields, many genetically produced products are already on the market. For example, the blood production factor erythropoietin has become vital for tens of thousands of people suffering from kidney disorders. Interferon alpha is being used successfully to treat certain kinds of cancers and jaundice. In these fields the innovation potential is high, since United States biotech firms alone now have about 300 new drugs which will soon be authorised. In the coming years every fourth new drug will be genetically produced. By and large, gene technology is already playing a very important role in research and development work on new drugs.

With gene technology, it has become possible to detect directly individual genes which in the course of a modification (mutation) are responsible for ill-nesses. This diagnosis of genetic material is performed especially if it is sus-pected that somebody is suffering from a particular illness or could contract it. Hereditary illnesses such as the mucous membrane disease cystic fibrosis can thus be identified in good time, *i.e.* diagnosed. The advantage of the procedure is that it is rapid and reliable. By diagnosing a hereditary predisposition early on, more successful treatment or prevention may be possible.

But the diagnosis of genetic material also makes it possible to identify predispositions to diseases which at the time of the diagnosis have not yet broken out. Some tests also simply investigate a heightened risk of a particular disease, such as colon cancer, being contracted at some time or another. A marked increase in such tests is expected in the years to come. In such cases a positive test does not say whether the disease will ever occur, which gives rise to serious questions:

- Should people be confronted with their genetic fate, even if they do not wish to hear about it?
- How can it be guaranteed that such tests are carried out on a voluntary basis only and with the patient's knowledge?
- Who should have access to such information, and for what purpose?
- How can data protection also be guaranteed for this kind of information?
- Is knowledge of one's future state of health equally tolerable to every individual?

While practical applications for drugs, vaccines and diagnostics already exist on the market, the use of new biotechnical methods for the development of artificial organs is still to a large extent in the experimental stage. The use of gene technology in connection with gene therapy, meaning its application to the treat-ment of body cells, is also still in an early, experimental phase. Its extensive use, for instance, in the treatment of cancer or AIDS is just as uncertain today as is the use of organs from genetically modified animals for transplants (xenotransplants).

GENOMICS – GIVING GENETIC INFORMATION A MEANING

The Human Genome Project is often described as the Manhattan Project of genetics. Deciphering the entire haploid genetic material of a human being is in fact a vast undertaking, with about 3 000 million characters to be decoded one by one. Although in 1996 only about 1 per cent of these data were available, the operation on which dozens of research groups are working worldwide is to be completed by the year 2005.

The American researcher Eric Lander has compared this project with the drawing up of the periodic table of chemical elements from 1869 to 1889. At the time, research chemists tried to group the different elements systematically. Today, however, it is not a matter of dealing with about 100 chemical elements but with about 100 000 genes. These genes, however, need only about 5 per cent of the entire genome. The other sequences in man's genetic endowment are possibly the flotsam and jetsam of the history of evolution, and therefore to a large extent of no importance to the body.

The governments of Europe, Japan and the United States support the Genome Project with around $250 million a year. The science involving research into genetic endowment is known as genomics. It is a multidisciplinary field. Physicists and engineers are developing machines so that work on decoding the genome can be automated and progress rapidly. Molecular biologists and geneticists classify the data and interpret them. Computer engineers work out programmes which give rapid access to the data and make it possible to compare different sequences within a reasonable time.

On the basis of the human genome sequence – meaning the entire sequence of characters – and further research, it will be possible to understand more clearly how human genes work. However, this will still not enable us to understand the nature of an individual. Genome research will therefore not produce for us a crystal-clear, transparent human being.

The Genome Project is of capital importance for the future of the pharmaceutical industry, since it will point the way to the causes and therefore to the treatment of many illnesses. Of the 30 000 illnesses that we know of today, only a few thousand can be treated. However, large sections of the population are affected by 100 to 150 of these illnesses. The origin of many of them is at least partly genetic, although often several genes are simultaneously involved. High blood pressure and other complex ailments are caused roughly by five to ten genes.

In medicine it is now known that there are slightly over 400 different targets for medication – enzymes, receptors and other biomolecules which can be blocked or otherwise influenced. Genomics opens up completely new horizons for treatment: approximately 3 000 to 10 000 new gene targets will be revealed by decoding the human genome and by the subsequent functional analysis.

If genes for new targets can be identified, and the way in which they interact can be understood, many possibilities will be opened up for new approaches to treatment. Today, the complexity of life and of pathological processes is still an obstacle to such an understanding.

It is expected that individualised treatment will be another consequence of genomics. Many medicines are not fully effective for all patients. Likewise, certain side-effects occur among some patients and not others. The cause of such differences often lies in the patient's genetic endowment. Different variants of genes exist, so that a specific group of drugs will be broken down by the body more slowly or more quickly in some cases than in others. If the substance is eliminated slowly, it remains longer in the body and thus has a different effect. With such knowledge it will become possible to classify the patient genetically with regard to his or her possible reaction to drugs, and therefore to optimise treatment.

INFECTIOUS DISEASES

Gene technology can make important contributions to better treatment, not only for diseases in which the patient's genetic predisposition is involved, but also in infectious diseases such as AIDS or malaria. When more research has been done on the molecular mechanisms triggering diseases – that is, when more is known about the details of the interaction between the pathogen and the host – it will be possible to develop new forms of treatment. For example, anti-HIV drugs are already on the market owing to the knowledge of the virus acquired from molecular biology research.

Resistance to drugs is also increasingly a problem owing to the accelerating use of antibiotics. In other words, more and more pathogens have become immune to many antibiotics. This problem is particularly marked in hospitals where bacteria can survive despite basic hygiene measures and become resistant. Tuberculosis (TB), for instance, is also increasingly reappearing in western countries. If it is not identified and treated in time, this disease can be fatal. In many Third World countries TB is the most common cause of death, and is therefore classified by the World Health Organisation (WHO) as one of the most dangerous infectious diseases. The cause of the epidemic in industrialised countries is often inappropriate treatment as well as the spread of Koch's bacilli which have built up many kinds of resistance to hitherto effective drugs.

Owing to their rapid multiplication and genetic plasticity, micro-organisms can adapt sometimes within weeks to an environment containing antibiotics. Pharmaceutical research is therefore engaged in a race against pathogens. Through research into molecular details of pathogens and their interaction with the human body, it is hoped that medicine will be able to take a substantial lead in this race.

FOOD

In addition to medicine, biotechnology and gene technology are mainly used at present in food production and processing. In the course of this century biotechnology has made great progress in both of these areas, mainly by developing and using traditional as well as new approaches. Artificial reproduction techniques in cattle breeding have boosted the trend. For many years now, artificial insemination has been routine practice in animal breeding.

Compared with the health field, modern biotechnology has opened up fewer really new approaches in this sector. The objectives in crop farming, animal breeding and food processing are not basically modified by the possibilities of gene technology. However, they do enable these objectives to be achieved more quickly and more efficiently. The influence of modern biotechnology with regard to animals, plants and food processing differs from one application sector to another.

In the case of farm animals there are two main goals – resistance to disease and increased yield. Transgenic animals which can be fed more efficiently and which put on less fat thanks to additional growth hormone genes have already been produced. But it is unlikely that the meat from these generally optimised animals w ll find its way onto our plates in the next few years – firstly, "designer nutrition" is at odds with the trend towards natural foodstuffs; secondly, in some cases gene technology applications are inconsistent with the protection of animals.

Many surveys also confirm that the public is against gene technology in connection with livestock. But gene technology has a future in the animal health field: genetically produced drugs, vaccines and diagnostics could help prevent animal diseases and treat them more effectively.

Alongside medical applications, gene technology has made the greatest progress in plant breeding. The cultivation of over two dozen genetically modified plants has been authorised worldwide. This number will increase sharply in the coming years, owing to the four main aims in plant breeding:

- *Modified plant quality*. The idea is to influence, for example, the nutritional content or shelf time. The famous anti-mush tomato known as Flavr-Savr does not rot so quickly as its untreated predecessor because it has been genetically modified.
- *Resistance to weed killers*. Round-up, for example, is a weed killer which is rapidly broken down in the soil; it therefore has ecological advantages over other herbicides. But food plants such as soya are also sensitive to Round-up and have died when treated with this product. Transgenic soya plants now have an additional resistance gene enabling them to survive treatment with Round-up.

- *Resistance to pests.* Several per cent of the world harvest is lost to pests, whether viruses, fungi or insects. It is possible to make crops resistant to such pests by modifying them genetically. Thus maize plants are protected against an insect, the maize pyralid, and potatoes against certain viruses.

- *Modified agronomic characteristics.* Plant research scientists turn to gene technology in order to extend the possibilities of crop farming, for example to areas which previously could not be cultivated. The aim is thereby to produce crops that can be grown on land with a very high salt content, or in very dry and warm regions.

Initial experience with transgenic plants such as maize, soya or rape show that these new strains have a better field performance than the traditional varieties. The agro-food industry forecasts annual growth rates in the next few years of 40 per cent in the sale of genetically modified seed. It is therefore to be expected that within a few decades all seed that is widely marketed will be influenced in one way or another by gene technology, whether the seed itself has been genetically modified or genetic manipulation methods have been used in the breeding phase for the selection of plants.

Widely developed traditional biotechnology techniques are often used today in food processing. This applies mainly to controlled microbiological processes as well as the use of technical enzymes and other additives obtained from microbial sources (vitamins, antioxidants, sweeteners, etc.). Milk thus curdles with the use of the rennet enzyme chymosin, and matures with the addition of special bacteria. In the last ten years many genetically produced enzymes for food processing have been marketed. Additives or sweeteners such as vitamins and aspartam are partly produced in genetically modified micro-organisms. It is expected that in the next few years modern biotechnology will mainly influence the development and production of new technical enzymes and additives.

Genetically modified bacteria for processing food (yoghurt, cheese, kefir, etc.) – which for example can protect themselves against virus attacks, secrete strawberry flavour into yoghurt, make cheese mature more quickly or ferment light beer – are now being studied and developed in laboratories and pilot facilities. Such applications greatly depend on consumer acceptance. At the present time, it cannot be foreseen how far genetically modified micro-organisms will be used in food processing.

In connection with the consumers' interests, it is important that foodstuffs produced by means of gene technology should be labelled to that effect. Labelling permits transparency as well as product choice, and is therefore demanded by the overwhelming majority of European consumers. It is still not certain what the labelling arrangements will be, for within a few years virtually all foodstuffs will probably be affected in some way by gene technology.

ENVIRONMENT/RAW MATERIALS

Environmental protection has assumed great importance in the course of the last decade. Biotechnology – alone or combined with chemical and physical methods – provides approaches to solutions for a series of environmental problems. It opens up new possibilities with regard to the provision of energy and raw materials, production, waste treatment and the remediation of contaminated sites. So far, however, biotechnology methods have been used in the environmental field in only a few cases, such as sewage treatment and the decontamination of land and soil. Some studies, however, forecast a growing and lucrative world market for biotechnology solutions in the environmental field.

For decades environmental technology has developed and improved disposal methods for waste, sewage and off-gas, as well as clean-up methods for soil and ground water. The limits to these technologies are becoming quite clear, considering the often expensive processes needed to treat large areas. From the ecological as well as economic viewpoint, end-of-pipe techniques should therefore be increasingly replaced or at least supplemented to a large extent by preventive techniques. This means that waste should already be avoided in the course of production, or at least substantially reduced. New functions are thus being set for environmental technology, such as the development of new, environment-friendly, waste-free or low-waste products, or new environmentally sound methods of using by-products and waste.

As in the health, agricultural and nutrition sectors, environmental technology will be increasingly confronted with the use of genetically optimised micro-organisms, for the results required can rarely be produced using traditional procedures and mixed cultures. Conventional treatment systems such as sewage plants, biofilters or composting use naturally enriched microbial mixed cultures in order to mineralise harmful substances. The efficiency and further technical development of these methods are affected by our limited knowledge of their basic biological processes. We still know too little about the ecological interactions among the multitude of micro-organisms and higher organisms involved, or about the basic biochemical, molecular biology or genetic principles of the most complex reaction sequences.

Gene technology improvements in such complex systems can only be expected in the long term, since the various degradation reactions have not been fully explained and are coded by a multitude of largely unknown genes. Experiments with recombinant organisms ("specialists") are therefore limited at present to pure cultures and laboratory tests. Genetically optimised organisms usually fail to stand up to the practical conditions encountered in a sewage plant or a contaminated soil. A genetically engineered improvement for the degradation of a specific harmful substance is not in itself sufficient for survival in the competitive pressure of the natural ecosystem. Recombinant micro-organisms surviving in a mixed culture also frequently lose their genetically engineered characteristics after a few generations.

Practical applications with recombinant organisms in conventional biological disposal processes therefore do not exist at present, and there is little probability that they will be seen in the near future. The right approach to improving strains by conventional processes should be produced by the many existing possibilities of modifying micro-organisms through selective adjustments and natural gene transfers. The fact that micro-organisms are extremely adaptable to new environmental conditions should show the way. Wherever there has been sufficient time for adaptation, optimally adjusted ecosystems have established themselves in nature.

BIOLOGICAL WEAPONS

Gene technology is also used in military laboratories that study and develop biological warfare agents or test defensive strategies (*e.g.* vaccination). Micro-organisms such as the anthrax agent, which are already known as biological weapons, are the focal point in biological warfare. Obviously little is known about research in this field. As in environmental technology, gene technology cannot be expected to do "better" than nature. It will hardly be possible for gene technology to produce more dangerous, more infectious or more aggressive micro-organisms than nature has done so far. But it is conceivable that the agents can be made more resistant and available for military use through gene technology, so that, for example, they will survive a bomb explosion.

BIOELECTRONICS/NEUROINFORMATICS

The bioelectronics concept applies to research concerning the analysis, generation, transfer and storage of signals in biological systems; it also includes the application of this knowledge to the development of biosensors and other bioelectronic components which, for example, could be used for the construction of completely new kinds of computers (biochips). In this sense, bioelectronics is a relatively young and interdisciplinary science bordering on (bio)chemistry, (bio)physics, molecular biology, biotechnology, nanotechnology and microelectronics.

Neuroinformatics is the term used to describe a special discipline which has emerged from the interaction between neurobiology and informatics. It focuses on theoretical and experimental research on information processing by the central nervous system and on biotechnology applications relating to the integration of electronic components and neural structures. Neuroinformatics is an interdisciplinary research field which includes the neurosciences, informatics, microelectronics and biotechnology.

Bioelectronics and neuroinformatics obviously have a vast scientific and technological innovation potential. However, in the present very early stage of development, statements about future technological innovation or economic significance are extremely speculative. Nothing more than approaches to market applications has been made; virtually all activities are limited to basic research. Bioelectronics and neuroinformatics are not mentioned at all in many biotechnology studies, presumably because the technologies are not yet sufficiently developed and are still seldom seen as part of the biotechnology picture. Great interest is being shown, however, in this research field owing to its vast innovation potential.

Biosensors are based on the direct coupling of a biologically active component, the signal transmitter, with a signal converter (transducer). A biosensor's selectivity with regard to the subject of analysis is determined by the appropriate biological identification process. Medical diagnosis and monitoring, environment and food analysis, and biological process checks are the current and possible future fields for biosensor applications.

Marked progress has been made in the last few decades in neurobiology and informatics (automatic data processing). Computers and smart systems are omnipresent in society and in the technology and scientific fields. Massively parallel systems, algorithms, and the attempt to emulate human capabilities in technical solutions using robotics, imaging techniques and expert systems are fascinating major intellectual challenges in the informatics field.

In the neurosciences field, an interdisciplinary attempt is being made to understand the structure and function of nervous systems. The neurosciences have strong traditional ties with medicine and the natural sciences. The tremendous increase in the number of innovative publications, such as the "Decade of the Brain" in the United States and the "Human Frontier Science Programme" (HFSP) in neurobiology, shows how sharply interest has focused on neurosciences. The greatest challenge here is to grasp, by means of quantitative theories, the functional implications at different levels of the already vast and rapidly increasing knowledge of information processing structures, and to relate these levels to one another.

Despite all that neurosciences and informatics have in common, there has been relatively little cross-fertilization in the past between them. There are many reasons for this. The specialists in the two fields did not have a sufficiently detailed knowledge of each others' problems and approaches to solutions. In addition, the "selection criteria" in both fields were quite different: in informatics the focus had to be on logical precision and efficiency, while in the neurosciences

– and especially in medical applications – it had to be on the results of evolution. Even when information technologists were studying brain functions in the artificial intelligence field, the objectives were quite different. In artificial intelligence, it was considered that the brain functions could be sufficiently explained by determining the mathematical algorithm, while neuroscientists often showed more interest in biological structures and considered research on algorithms as premature.

However, the gap between neurobiology and information technology is narrowing:

- First, the fine parallelism of analog "artificial neural networks" (ANN) is becoming increasingly important in computer science as a theoretically and technically advantageous alternative to the "rough" parallelism of digital computers.

- A second basic reason is the access to rapid and lower-cost workstations and high-performance microprocessors.

- Third, intriguing joint applications combining neuroscience, nanotechnology and informatics are emerging in biotechnology, with the interaction between microprocessors and the nervous system: neural prostheses have already proved successful in some cases of hearing failure in which acoustic signals can be transferred to the brain by stimulating hearing nerves. Motor activity can also be produced by functional stimulation of the muscles, and sensorial signals can be detected on peripheral nerves and decoded by adaptive computer programmes. A "smart" prosthesis for paraplegics could be produced by integrating these components in a sensorial motor control instrument, which could be implanted like a pacemaker if the connections are reliable enough.

Current computer concepts are based on silicon chip technology. Owing to final storage capacities, the development of smaller and more efficient chips has natural limits which will be reached in the near future. Various (bio)molecules will serve as electronic components in futuristic alternative concepts. It is claimed that real biochips will be produced through self-organisation of the molecular electronic components; initial two-dimensional arrangements will subsequently be selectively networked to form three-dimensional molecular structures. So far, biochips have simply been interesting intellectual concepts.

THE RISK DEBATE AND SAFETY GUIDELINES

The possible risks in gene technology became a subject of debate among research scientists at the start of the 1970s, shortly after the first experiments involving *in vitro* recombination of genes. Some of the researchers taking part in these discussions were using gene technology strategies to investigate the characteristics of carcinogenic viruses. The aim was therefore to prevent the researchers from being infected with cancer genes themselves. The risk debate in the early years therefore centred mainly on personnel safety.

Today the focus in safety research is increasingly on issues connected with the economic application of gene technology. The debate is centred on risks relating to genetically modified micro-organisms on the one hand, and to plants on the other. The main concerns are the impact on human health (infections, tumours, allergies, poisoning, greater resistance to antibiotics) and on the environment (new kinds of weeds, ousting of other species from an ecosystem, impairment of biodiversity, poisoning of animals).

Although all nations engaged in advanced research entered the risk debate early on, much of the discussion took place within the United States, where the Asilomar Conference was held in February 1975. At this conference, which in the meantime has become legendary, a distinction was mainly drawn between two types of risks: the possibly pathogenic effects on researchers and their environment, and the longer-term uncertainty as to how the environment would react to the release of organisms with a genetically modified genome.

The scientific community developed binding guidelines for gene technology in order to contain these risks. The United Kingdom and the United States in particular took the lead, and the guidelines were very soon harmonized at international level. This phase of self-regulation in the scientific field was followed in the 1980s and 1990s in many countries by statutory regulation.

Statutory provisions have now been adopted in most countries working on gene technology, and to a large extent they have been harmonized. Thus genetically modified plants must be tested first in a laboratory, then in a greenhouse and finally in an open field, subject to government approval. Genetically modified plants are now investigated more thoroughly than untreated plant varieties due to a number of concerns, for example the risk that artificially inserted genes might be spontaneously transferred to other plants in the natural environment and therefore trigger ecological damage.

Although researchers have been able to prove in field trials that such genes could in fact be transferred to other plants, the transgenic plants released have so far not caused any damage. Gene transfer from one plant to another is a natural process which applies to conventional as well as inserted genes. Nor is there as yet any firm evidence that a transgenic plant will produce poisonous substances or trigger unexpected allergies.

From the biological viewpoint, foodstuffs provide the amino acids, vitamins and other important organic compounds needed in the body, as well as the energy and basic chemical components for the body's metabolism. Gene technology in no way affects this, either. As regards amino acids, the basic components for proteins, the human organism can produce only less than half of them by itself. The body must obtain the rest of these so-called essential amino acids from food by breaking proteins down. Genetically modified proteins consist of precisely the same 20 amino acids as traditional proteins. Therefore in principle, no new risks are to be expected.

If no damage has yet occurred, however, that does not mean that this will always be the case. Transgenic plants have been on the market only a few years, and the effects of cultivation and consumption over a long period are not yet known. It is possible that ecological damage will occur only after ten, twenty or thirty years. For this reason, long-term monitoring studies are being conducted on transgenic crops all over the world.

There is no reason either for sounding the all-clear with regard to research scientists in their laboratories: responsible researchers still consider it important to study any possible risks involved in research projects, to show due care and to keep to the binding guidelines. But on the whole, fewer ecological risks can be expected by inserting a well-known gene into a well-investigated plant than by introducing a plant from another environment in another continent, as has been the case for centuries with many edible and ornamental plants.

Only ten years ago the focus in the debate was still on technical safety issues. Now, social, policy and moral issues connected with the spread of gene technology in our society are becoming increasingly important. In the last few years modern biotechnology has frequently been the subject of technology assessment studies. Their objective is not only to determine the consequences of the technology from the economic and technical viewpoints, but also, by taking varied approaches, to give a comprehensive view of the consequences of a technical development, and therefore to provide a basis for policy and economic decisions. In most industrialised countries, technology assessment seems to be establishing itself as an instrument for policy counselling and technology planning. Risk appraisal will have an important place in this process, but will no longer be the focal point with regard to a new technology.

A BROADER CONCEPTION OF LIFE

Molecular genetics and the derived gene technology provide new, forceful inputs for a deeper understanding of vital functions and potential applications for the benefit of humanity. As many scientists say, enhanced knowledge of vital functions also strengthens respect for life. In turn this can lead to a greater awareness of our responsibilities towards nature. Gene technology contributes to a better understanding of ourselves and our environment; it is the interface between biological evolution and mankind's cultural evolution. Many experimental approaches in gene technology more or less imitate small steps in the evolution of organisms. The possible consequences of each of these steps must be assessed. The understanding of molecular developments in the process of biological evolution can thus be extremely helpful to us.

Studies on biological evolution by means of gene technology show that a large number of specific genes are the driving forces behind evolution, but they also show that these genes cannot determine its course. That statement may seem contradictory, but close examination reveals that these genes do not rigidly control vital functions. On the contrary, their impact is greatly marked by flexibility. They are in continual contact with environmental influences – a fact which even comes as a surprise to many molecular biologists and biochemists. Greater awareness of this fact on our part can certainly help to dispel our fears about the risks of gene technology. For ultimately the aim is to use this technology for the benefit of our civilisation and for the conservation of our animate and inanimate environment.

5

TECHNOLOGICAL DEVELOPMENT AND ORGANISATIONAL CHANGE: DIFFERING PATTERNS OF INNOVATION

by

Meinolf Dierkes, Jeanette Hofmann and Lutz Marz
Wissenschaftszentrum Berlin für Sozialforschung (WZB), Germany

CRISIS OF MODERNITY, TECHNOLOGY AND CHANGE

If discussion in the highly industrialised countries has come to focus increasingly on the future, the approaching and heavily symbolic change of the millennium counts as only part of the reason. Growing interest in what the future holds in store is attributable less to the number 2000 and the transition to the 21st century than to the pervasive and deep-seated crisis that modern societies are currently undergoing.

During the postwar decades, which have increasingly been referred to as the "golden age" (Glyn, Hughes, Lipietz and Singh, 1990) or the "thirty glorious years" (Fourastié, 1979), people in most of these countries were apt to take the extraordinary prosperity and stability of the times as a natural and abiding state of the socio-economic system. And against the backdrop of the American way of life, the German economic miracle, and the Swedish *Folkhem*, the mounting signs since the late 1960s that West Germany's golden age was on the wane were initially interpreted as intermittent aberrations that could always be remedied. The collapse of socialism in the late 1980s seemed to confirm this view, luring some observers, Francis Fukuyama for one, to assume that these new circumstances were not only enduring but eternal and that the "end of history" had been reached (Fukuyama, 1992; for a critique of this view, see Derrida, 1996).

However, a great deal of evidence now indicates that the glorious years may have passed, at least for the time being, and that a critical period has set in. In the social sciences it is described in various terms: the "great crisis" (Boyer, 1986, pp. 226-34), a "crisis of form" (Altvater, 1991), a "crisis of paradigm" (Dierkes, 1997, pp. 47-48), a "crisis of working society" (Offe, 1984, p. 7), a "crisis of organised modernism" (Wagner, 1995) and a "crisis of the welfare state" (Dierkes and Zimmermann, 1996). In these different analyses, two convictions clearly surface again and again. First, the crisis – as diagnosed – is both fundamental and persistent, and its future course and outcome cannot be foreseen at this time. Second, the crisis affects all institutions of society, from business organisations, unions, associations and federations to the state, political parties and the universities. If this assessment is true, then organisations must gird up for a lengthy interval of turbulence, one that may challenge their very *raison d'être* (Baecker, 1997).

For organisations, the burgeoning crisis is being felt at three different, but increasingly interrelated, levels. One is the change in the environment of organisations, to which they must adapt in order to ensure their existence (Dierkes, 1994). Another level lies within the organisations themselves. The crisis is not detouring around them; it is instead going right through them. In other words, it always engulfs organised space as well, though not always to the same depth and breadth from one instance to the next (Dierkes and Marz, 1998). Lastly, the present crisis is leading to an erosion and in many cases the subsequent disintegration of the individual organisation's learning conventions, that is, the time-tested internal consensus on what and how its members have to learn in order to cope with new and profoundly different environmental conditions (Dierkes and Marz, 1998).

Not surprisingly, many individuals and groups today thus sense the future to be much more uncertain than was the case just a decade or two ago. Much of what was then widely regarded as a technological, social, or political impossibility or even science fiction is now part of everyday life. More than a few people voice concern about how their work environments and their daily lives will change in the coming years. Equally unsurprising is that the issue of technological change and its likely impacts always plays a role in this complex discourse about the future.

The amazing aspect, however, at least from a social science perspective, is that many debates suffer from a classical misconception widely thought to have been eliminated – the explicit or inexplicit belief that technological change ultimately determines, overshadows, and dominates social change. The concept of cultural lag, which suggests that social systems need time to adjust to technological developments, is but the oldest and most prominent example of this view.

This perception of the relationship between technological and organisational change is also articulated in many other, sometimes spectacular ways, an obvious instance being the scenarios developed by the American robotics expert Hans Moravec in his book *Mind Children* (1990). Moravec saw a "genetic changing of the guard" (p. 13) in the first third of the 21st century, a transition in which evolution will be decoupled from its biological foundations as computers liberate the human mind from its protean "brawn" (p. 163) and endow it with eternal life in their computer hardware. Of course, such forays of the imagination are less the basis of serious, scientifically grounded scenarios and more the stuff of sci-fi films such as James Cameron's *The Terminator* or Paul Verhoeven's *Robocop*, in which human-and-machine hybrids dominate fear. Nevertheless, the attention that prophecies of this kind attract even among experts is sometimes quite notable. In Germany, for example, Moravec's book caused a stir for several years in an interdisciplinary discourse in which natural, social, and technology scientists focused on the social impacts of artificial intelligence (Marz, 1993a, b).

But technological determinism is not confined to extremes in which it takes on graphic form. It is usually manifested in much more subtle ways that often influence the thinking of people without their always being aware of it. For example, characterising the development of the information and communication technologies as the "digital revolution" (Coy, 1994) and speaking of a "digital Faust" (Bolter, 1990) may be incisive and catchy, but expressions of this sort can easily obscure the intricate interaction between technical and organisational change. They give the subliminal and often unintended impression that digitalisation *per se* is the engine of all change. But developments like "hypermedia" (Coy, 1994), "open computer networks" (Helmers, Hoffmann and Hofmann, 1996a) and "cyberspace" (Rheingold, 1992) as well as profound related visions like "world simulation" (Grassmuck, 1995) show that the specific features and directions of change cannot be conveyed by the cachets of digitalisation.

Visions like the "virtual organisation" also vividly demonstrate this point. Global computer networks already enable companies to interlink every aspect of the timing, substance, and communications of product development processes that cover the entire globe. These networks not only represent a system for transporting data but make it possible to create virtual space in which products and services are offered and sold worldwide or in which people widely separated in space can interact and communicate with each other in real time, allowing new forms of inter- and intra-organisational co-operation. Making use of the development potential is not just a problem of digitalisation. Wide-band data networks, high-speed computers and other technologies are indeed necessary but by no means sufficient if the virtual organisation is actually to be created and sustained.

In short, technological opportunities deriving from the results of autonomous and curiosity-driven basic research in the natural sciences are seen as agents that shape social and environmental conditions – and that view has shaped our concept of technology assessment. The objective is to investigate as many of the social, ecological, cultural, economic and political impacts of technologies as possible. The ultimate intention is to minimise negative impacts and maximise consequences regarded as desirable. Much of the research done in this context throughout the world proved helpful to decision-makers dealing with the impacts of new technologies. However, most of the research came too late to significantly modify the technology under consideration. Thus, most of the negative consequences had to be accepted or were at best only slightly mitigated. Efforts to go beyond simple technological determinism have therefore been undertaken over the last decade. Attempts to enhance the understanding of new technologies are under way in the hope of influencing the process of technological development itself, preferably when it is in an early, still formative state.

It goes without saying, however, that the interplay of technical and organisational change precludes understanding if one misconception is merely substituted for another, if technological determinism is replaced by some kind of social determinism in which the relative dominance of and relations between cause and effect are simply reversed. In the final analysis, determinisms like that boil down to the familiar and unproductive question of "Which came first, the chicken or the egg?" Studies on large technical systems (La Porte, 1991; Joerges, 1993; Mayntz, 1993) and on theories of actor networks (Akrich, 1992; Callon, 1991; Law, 1992) have made it increasingly clear that any conception will fail to adequately grasp the specific dynamics of present change, and will only lead to a number of fundamental paradoxes and unsatisfactory explanatory approaches, if it presents the technical and social aspects of that change solely, or even primarily, as more or less mutually opposed, independent spheres of action (Bijker and Law, 1992, pp. 290-306; Jasanoff, 1995; Latour, 1995).

One possibility for overcoming the misconception of technological and social determinism and for opening analytical perspectives on the processes of current changes is offered by a conceptual framework developed as part of social science research on technology development (Dierkes, 1993; Dierkes and Hoffmann, 1992; NRC, 1988). This approach is supported by findings, most dating from the last two decades,

> on the reverse side of the technology-society coin: the institutional shaping of technology. An accumulation of historical studies have now analyzed the way that dominant forces in society, including cultural settings, values, ideologies, and political and economic structures, [have] conditioned the development and introduction of new technology and the emergence of entire industrial systems. (NRC, 1988, p. 145)

In response to these findings, the study of technology has been undergoing a significant transformation during the past decade.

> The relation of technology to society has been reconsidered, and the conventional assumption that technological change is subject to a purely technical logic or economic imperative has been challenged. The design and the "technical" content of artifacts and systems are now seen to be amenable to social science analyses and explanation. Technology is deeply affected by

the context in which it is developed and used. Every stage in the generation and implementation of new technology involves a set of choices between different options. A range of interrelated factors – economic, social, cultural, political, organisational – affect which options are selected. Thus, a field of research has emerged where scholars from a wide variety of backgrounds seek to increase the understanding of technological development as a social process. (Dierkes and Hoffmann, 1992, p. 6)

Research based on this conceptual approach has focused on a wide range of particular areas, such as engine, writing, and telephone technologies (Buhr and Knie, 1993; Canzler, 1996; Canzler and Knie, 1994; Rogers, 1990); biotechnology and genetic engineering (Barben, 1997); artificial intelligence (Dierkes, 1994; Marz, 1993a, b); and communications and information technologies (Canzler, Helmers and Hoffmann, 1995; Grote, Helmers, Hoffmann and Hofmann, 1994); as well as general technological issues such as the connection between visions of technology and user interests (Hofmann, 1996, 1997) and the link between policy and technology development (Dierkes, Canzler, Marz and Knie, 1995; Hoffmann and Marz, 1992). These analyses have also focused on the significance those visions have for the development of regions (Krupp, 1995) and business corporations (Dierkes and Marz, 1994).

ORGANISATIONAL AND INSTITUTIONAL FACTORS SHAPING TECHNOLOGICAL DEVELOPMENT: A CONCEPTUAL BASIS

Building on the empirical findings of this broad range of studies, it is possible to construct a theoretical framework enabling researchers to elaborate the organisational and cultural factors that shape technological developments. According to the theoretical concept underlying that research, the drive to produce new technologies must be understood as an active social and political process (Dierkes, 1990). From the organisational point of view, several elements influencing the creation of new technologies can be identified. The three most important are examined in this context: visions, organisational culture, and organisational learning.

The role of visions in technology development

Visions describe ideas about future technologies shared by communities of individuals, institutions, and organisations involved in the research and development process (Dierkes, Hoffmann and Marz, 1996). They take the common understanding of the ideas' desirability and feasibility and project them into the not-too-distant future. These visions therefore become flexible and dynamic goals that exert great influence on the direction of innovation processes. They shape the complex multi-actor process of making decisions on whether to pursue certain technological options and eliminate others in research and development efforts (Dierkes and Marz, 1994).

Assuming that visions owe their considerable effectiveness and persuasiveness to something other than their "buzzword" character as a telegraphic grammatical form, one wonders where they get their strength. Popular visions such as the "information superhighway," the "cashless society" or the "paperless office" bundle institutions with experience and knowledge of the individuals involved, combining in a special and rather effective way what is feasible with what is desired. They do not promote or favour either view at the expense of the other but work instead to meld both aspirations as a common goal or understanding, crystallising them into a vivid and dynamic new shape.

Such visions of technological developments serve a threefold function: they provide orientation, facilitate co-ordination, and stimulate motivation. In their orienting function, they provide a reference point to which individuals can focus their perception, thought, and decision-making processes in a way that effectively establishes a common objective for thoughts about the future. This future objective, or reference point, involves individual aspirations, expectations and hopes that appear obtainable not because individuals simply desire them to be so but because they are grounded in the individuals' perception of their feasibility in the near future. Visions form the basis of specific and vivid perceptions that combine concrete memories and ideas often collected over years or even decades of experience with deeply rooted and often highly diverse personal convictions, fears, prejudices and commitments.

Visions not only unveil new future horizons and perceptions, but also co-ordinate – as the second function – perceptions, thoughts, and decision-making processes to establish a basic understanding among individuals and organisations. The existence of this common ground is especially significant in providing a platform where experts and laypersons can meet, overcoming what are often vastly different frames of references, and significantly simplifying the required co-operation between these two groups.

Visions also serve a motivational function in that such ideas or perceptions are present in both the minds and hearts of individuals. Typical visions, such as the "manless factory" or the "nuclear society", often stir strong emotional responses within individuals. These visions do not just appeal to individuals' rational or objective calculations but draw upon those norms and values that lie at the root of the individual's perceptions, thoughts and decisions. It is this aspect that accounts for the profound ability of visions to awaken interest within an individual and motivate that person into action.

The role of organisational culture in technology development

The influence of visions on technological developments is strongly filtered by an organisation's culture. Organisational culture can best be defined as various social or normative means that bind the members of an organisation together; contribute to common values, ideas or perspectives; and come to be reflected in what are often symbolic ways such as myths, rituals, stories and language. Culture influences, among other things, the manner in which the organisation and its members perceive their environment and changes in it, how they define their role regarding the environment, and what individual and collective behaviour is considered desirable and legitimate. Organisational culture is both all-encompassing and very specific. It is rooted in an organisation's specific, nontransferable historical development within which the relation between members, their perceptions, their decisions, and their behavioural patterns are affected and formed (Dierkes, 1988).

Organisational culture can be both a strength and a weakness to organisations. It provides a sense of stability and identity to which the members can refer while also saddling the organisation with a pattern of behaviour that was successful in the past but might be inappropriate or even impede efforts to cope with current challenges (Dierkes, Hähner and Berthoin-Antal, 1997).

The role of organisational learning in technology development

Similarly, organisational learning plays a key role in the development of technologies by virtue of its ability to influence the direction and course of research and development within an organisation or in a network of organisations. In contrast to individual or group learning, organisational learning is defined as the collective acquisition or activation of new prevailing perceptions, strategic competencies or thought processes in response to a changing external environment (Dierkes and Hähner, 1994; Pawlowsky, 1994). Learning, as the term is used in this context, does not mean skills-oriented or conventional classroom learning but rather the development of a flexible response to or anticipation of change by an organisation as a whole. This learning is embodied in areas such as the courage to move away from old strategies and management concepts in order to discover and promote new or modified organisational behaviour and to encourage new thought processes. Reflected in new perceptions or observations, defensive goals or opportune visions, organisational learning challenges, and often changes, existing structures and cultures.

The need to learn has increasingly become an element critical to the success of organisations (Dierkes and Hähner, 1994). Many have developed their culture, structure and leadership in a relatively stable environment that provided a clear overview of a particular product market, field of technology or industrial sector.

The dynamic changes now affecting those markets require organisations to re-evaluate their perceptions, values and behaviour, often extensively, so that they can react quickly to new global competition. They must develop long-range strategies that encompass new forms of production processes or new products and services. Should this self-evaluation occur too slowly, an organisation runs the risk of "missing the boat" for market changes or developments in technology, and may find it impossible to maintain a competitive position (Dierkes, 1992).

Organisational learning is found in, and often brought about by, individuals and groups. However, because it is not simply a collection of discrete learning experiences but rather the collective acquisition of new perceptions or competencies, it can actually be *less* than the sum of individual learning found within an organisation – in other words, not all of the perceptions and competencies gained by individuals are transferable to the organisation as a whole. On the other hand, organisational learning is often *greater* than collective individual learning, for it has the ability to combine and magnify the learning effects of individuals' knowledge and experiences through daily co-operation and communication processes.

The structures for developing new ideas and realising new innovation potential vary from company to company, in some cases considerably. At one extreme, R&D in some firms is separated from daily operations in order to maximise freedom and creativity. In firms at the other extreme, R&D may be closely tied to daily operations in order to ensure that products are relevant in research applications (Dierkes, 1985).

As the following two case examples illustrate, all three factors outlined above – visions, organisational cultures and organisational learning – can exert a lasting influence on the intricate interplay of technological and organisational change. The examples have two aspects in common. First, they both refer to a particular kind of technological change: the new information and communication technologies that have been emerging since the mid-1960s, specifically the computerisation and digitalisation of daily worlds. Second, both cases clearly show why thinking only in terms of technological or social determinism can shift and distort the perspective on future development.

THE PERSISTENCE OF THE AUTOMOTIVE SOCIETY: INNOVATIONS WITHOUT MAJOR SOCIAL AND INSTITUTIONAL CHANGE

In contrast to visions specific to particular organisations or companies, the vision of the automotive society has much broader and deeper moorings. It is not rooted in just one organisation but rather in the companies of the automotive industry, governments, automobile associations and areas outside the organisational sphere, such as the daily behaviour of drivers and their individual and collective projections of what is desirable and feasible (Canzler, 1996; Canzler and

Marz, 1997). This vision, through which the automobile dominates thinking about mobility, has structured and controlled transport policies for decades and can easily be seen as one of the most successful technological visions in terms of range, stability, and long-term impact (Dierkes, Canzler, Marz and Knie, 1995).

For many years the automobile was the undisputed symbol and indicator of individual and macrosocial prosperity, as reflected in the statement "What is good for General Motors is good for America", or in the Volkswagen beetle, which for many years served as the emblem of the German economic miracle. Despite numerous pressures and trends that indicate a restructuring of the automotive society (Canzler and Knie, 1994), a profound conversion is not in sight (Dierkes, Buhr, Canzler and Knie, 1995). The automobile has many problems, but it has lost little or none of its attraction (Canzler, 1996).

Throughout the world, the vision of the automotive society is presently so powerful that its influence suffuses nearly every organisation involved in it. It is expressed as learning that systematically draws on past experience. In this context the escalating crisis of mobility centred on the car, especially in large metropolitan areas, is treated as though it were a variant of earlier, successfully managed crises. (On the few exceptions to this experiential learning, see Knie, 1994, 1997.) The learning experience in this case is fixated particularly on clinging to, but technically upgrading, the core of the automobile vision – the "high-performance, internal combustion limousine" (Canzler and Knie, 1994).

A major surge of innovation expected from the use of new technologies hitherto having nothing to do with cars will likely do much to entrench the automotive society and even expand it throughout the world. High hopes are attached to incorporating information and sensory technology as well as optoelectronics into the automobile of the future. The actual increase in efficiency to be gained through accessories that use information technology is occasionally overestimated, but there is no reason to underestimate their potential capacity to solve some of the automotive society's current major problems. Presumably, telematics has great capacity to modernise the transport sector, a view reflected in the PROMETHEUS project and other research funding programmes, especially in Europe. The networked and intelligent car is the central element in a vision of the automotive society in the future.

The vehicle of the future is expected to bring three kinds of relief from the negative impacts of the automotive society (Canzler, 1996). First, collective traffic information systems (bulletins on traffic conditions and parking availability) and individual traffic routing systems à la autopilot or scout are supposed to improve the efficiency with which existing roads and parking spaces are used, thereby increasing the capacity of the infrastructure that serves motor vehicles. Static CD-ROM directional systems are increasingly being supplemented by satellite-aided global positioning systems (GPS) and information systems capable of reporting changes in traffic conditions (*e.g.* accidents, congestion and roadworks) almost as soon as they occur so that they can be calculated into directions about which route to take.

Second, continued development and integration of information technology is intended to lead to what are called pretravel information systems. Available online through the PC in one's home, they are to aid the planning of journeys immensely and relieve today's rush-hour conditions by finally expanding the quality and amount of information available to people before they set out. A hitherto unknown degree of certainty in one's planning seems close at hand.

Third, there are plans to control the times and volumes of traffic by electronic road (or congestion) pricing. Electronic tolls and electronic restrictions to access are not infrequently regarded as a way of introducing market principle into the use of the transport infrastructure. In addition, increased safety is expected because interactive systems in road vehicles can be used for emergencies, too.

Given the direction of these technical developments, perhaps the best term for them is stagnating innovation, innovative stagnation – or simply, stagnovation (Canzler and Marz, 1997). This technological change does not mean that decades-old structures of mobility have simply been preserved or frozen, or that they are being completely reshaped or even overcome. The technical innovations clearly represent learning and adaptation by the organisations and institutions involved, or at least partial learning. They are innovative in that a broad spectrum of new information and communications technologies is brought to bear in order to stabilize the existing vision of the automotive society and exploit the given, but narrow, scope of action to the utmost. Bringing the global data network into the high-performance limousine creates both virtual and real space for these innovations within the realm of the existing powerful vision. However, these technical developments are stagnating in the sense that innovation will not be able to abolish the relevant problems of the automotive society; it primarily postpones or temporarily relieves them by making it possible to manage them more efficiently. Using computers to break up traffic congestion will delay the total breakdown of the transport system in metropolitan areas, but will not eliminate its causes.

As innovation is often significant within the realm of a powerful dominant technological vision, it tends to reinforce stagnovation, thereby postponing the systematic search for and promotion of new technological visions. Postponing the problems of automotive mobility gains time in the short and medium terms. But what is this opportunity being used for – to solve the problems in the long run or merely to hold them in abeyance? Stagnovation decreases the chances of fundamental modernisation by concentrating innovation potential on prolonging the life span of currently dominant technological visions and by not equally promoting the development of new ways to tackle the underlying problems. The longer this trend persists, the harder it will be to find and tread alternative paths of technological development that enhance mobility in a different social and organisational context. Therefore, the greatest danger of stagnovation is that it masks the relation between postponing a problem and exacerbating it, thereby encouraging a lackadaisical and naive attitude "that things will work out when the time comes".

Given these innovation strategies that prolong the life span of a dominant technological vision through partial learning and limited organisational change, the question is whether stagnovation is only a peculiarity of the automotive society or whether this phenomenon lurks in other practices for coping with crises. If stagnovation does exist in cases of technological visions, then it is essential to understand the roots of such a strategy, for widespread stagnovation processes are a prime source of a sociopsychological climate that complicates the effort to cope productively with the crisis besetting modern society.

Perhaps the most apt, if slightly overstated, expression for this climate is manic-depressive. On the one hand, stagnovation promotes feelings of euphoria. The more successfully innovation delays basic problems of modernisation, the greater the danger that partial postponement of problems will be taken for general solutions. Grouting traditional structures with incremental innovations appears to be *the* way to surmount crises. The actors of stagnovation can gain the heady impression that the worst is over, or at least that everything is under control. On the other hand, stagnovation fosters feelings of depression. Despite many assurances to the contrary, the postponement of far-reaching modernisation through stagnovation creates a vague sense of unease in people. It is becoming ever more difficult for those involved in the definition of technological development to avoid admitting that continuation is not ultimately progress. At the same time, the concentration on modernising and extending the sidetracks diverts attention from possible, though arduous, ways out of the growing problems. The strategy of fixing the problem but not solving it, which is embedded in partial learning within the framework of dominant technological visions, will appear more and more inescapable. The sense of stagnovation's meaninglessness in the long run and the impression of its inescapability are most likely what nurture the latent depression associated with stagnovation.

In light of stagnovation, one naturally asks whether there are other, alternative paths of development along which new information and communication technologies are used to induce social innovation rather than simply to preserve and incrementally modernise traditional social alliances. It becomes immediately clear that such paths do exist when one turns to a field in which technical and social innovations and changes intertwine and foster each other, as is currently the case with the Internet.

INNOVATION THROUGH CO-OPERATION AMONG COMPETITORS: THE INTERNET

As the second example of the interplay of technological and organisational change, the Internet illustrates how technological innovations inadvertently pave the way for new forms of production and organisation that, in turn, exert recognisable influence on the further development of technology. Because of the history of the Internet's emergence, its special transmission technology has become an international development project involving nearly all major manufacturers of the information and communications industry. Companies that compete for market shares when selling their products are co-operating intensely and successfully when it comes to technological innovations in the Internet. How is that possible? What are the conditions of this collaboration?

It is well known that the Internet was originally a product of research funded by the state. Development of the basic transmission principles that distinguish the Internet from the world of the telephone (including the packet-switching principle of transmission and the unreliable best-effort service) was first financed by the US Department of Defense, and later increasingly by the National Science Foundation (Cerf, 1993). For that reason the Internet was still a research network in both senses until the early 1990s. The developers and key user groups of the technology were scientists, most of whom were based at universities. With few exceptions, such as Bolt, Beranek, and Newman (BBN), it was the computer centres of American universities that were interlinked in ARPANET, Internet's forerunner (Comer, 1991; Huitema, 1995).

The significance of those roots in the culture of academia for the way in which Internet-related technological development is organised lies primarily in the scientific nature of the innovation in question. Unlike the rules of the game in business, one of the irrevocable tenets of the culture of the academic community is that research results are published and offered for discussion. What is new is shared; it is made available to others. Accordingly, the transmission technologies on which the Internet is built today originated as a collaborative project involving what was originally a small group of physicists and engineers, some of whom had not even completed their university degrees. Dividing work among them, they developed, tested and implemented new ideas intended to facilitate the exchange of data between computers (Hafner and Lyon, 1996; Salus, 1995; RFC 1000, 1987). The culture of open discussion is documented not least by the archived series of publications that fostered the exchange of information: the Internet Engineering Notes (IEN) and the Requests for Comments (RFC); the latter still exist today. The Internet's transmission and user standards are made public as RFCs, "the archive of the Net's wisdom" (Huitema, 1995, p. 19).

The advent of such typical Internet services as file transfer, e-mail and mailing lists spurred the Internet's development from a focus of research to a research resource. As one of the engineers involved has put it, "There is a tremendous potential in using the Internet to 're-invent' the Net. The Internet model is being applied to the Internet itself to explore new ways to expand the Net" (S. Doran, 17 April 1996, on the "IPv6 haters" mailing list). The distribution of communication via mailing lists, which makes it possible to send messages to as many receivers as desired, is the most important instrument of discussion and co-operation in the Internet's development today. The related technology is developing publicly and, in the vast majority of cases, decentrally *via* the Internet (Crocker, 1993; RFC 2026, 1996). Worldwide electronic archives available to anyone ensure that discussion articles and technical specifications become accessible as part of the historical record.

As the Internet expanded beyond the research world, the work on its development slowly formalized. In 1986 the Internet Engineering Task Force (IETF), an open institution without legal status, was formed to help place the ongoing development of the Internet on a new organisational footing (Lehr, 1995).

The gradual withdrawal of government funding for the Internet development was more than offset by ever-greater financial commitment from the business community. This involvement initially came to the attention of the Internet's developers because an increasing number of the active members were leaving the university for the business world. Over the same period, the IETF began to grow considerably, a process that continues today. A look at the e-mail addresses of the active Internet engineers shows that few senders are from a university these days. Harvard University, MIT, Stanford, the University of Southern California and the University of California at Los Angeles (UCLA), once centres of Internet development, have ceded their leading role in this area to the manufacturers of computers and network technologies, the major users, and the providers who organise access to the Internet. Visiting the triannual meeting of the IETF, one does still run into many veterans and heroes of the 1960s and early 1970s in their T-shirts and sandals, but their ID badges meanwhile sport the names of companies, most of which are younger than the Net itself. Firms like FTP Software, Cybercash, RWhois, Openroute and Netweek allude to Internet services and technical functions that did not exist until just a few years ago, such as the World Wide Web.

The Internet's growth is reflected not only in the rising number of users, but also in the birth of new markets and the many new companies that have been founded to serve them. Netscape, the world-renowned manufacturer of browsers, the device with which one navigates through the graphic world of the World Wide Web, is just one example. Another is UUNET, which has meanwhile become the world's largest provider. These changes are paralleled by the emergence of new areas of business activity, especially in the telecommunications industry, that send network specialists to the IETF's working meetings.

The business community's burgeoning interest in the Internet has made those meetings major events. Whereas fewer than 100 people attended them in the mid-1980s,[1] that many participants are now sent by just one company, such as Cisco, BBN, or Sun Microsystems. IETF meetings attended by 1 500 to 2 000 participants are meanwhile no exception, for they are essential for any company that is or wants to be active in the Internet area. In the workaday world, too, the active members are largely occupied with "voluntarily" collaborating on the development of new Internet technologies that can be standardized.[2] Many active Internet developers spend much of their available work time writing Internet drafts, reading mailing lists, and discussing current issues, yet these same engineers are now in great demand. They are specialists who can pick and choose their employers.

The IETF's change from an academic research community to an international and largely commercial platform for the continued development of the Internet has been gradual. Today, it is the most important technological and economic body for the development of new network technologies. The global expansion of the Internet bears witness to the superiority of this institution's procedures and products over such other bodies as the International Organization for Standardization (ISO) (Genschel, 1995). Yet how is it possible for competing companies to collaborate so productively?

A plausible explanation is rooted in the special mixture of procedural, cultural, and product-centred characteristics of this model of co-operation. One important procedural aspect has already been mentioned: the academic community's rules of the game, which have provided a culture and structure of open co-operation in the Internet ever since its early phase of development. Unlike the ISO and other standard-setting institutions, the IETF has remained open to all individuals interested in contributing. Neither membership nor representation is formally regulated. Anyone is welcome if they have the necessary technical expertise (Helmers, Hoffmann and Hofmann, 1996*a*, *b*; RFC 2026, 1996). And each person speaks only for him- or herself – that is, only technical arguments, not economic or political power, are accepted for advancing one's standpoint as a key element of the Internet's culture base.

This aspect touches also on the cultural dimension facilitating the co-operation between companies. The well-respected individuals in the IEFT are those who not only possess great technical competence but who also make it plain to everyone involved that they are able to distinguish between the vested interests of their employers and the interest in the Internet as a common good. The goal uniting everyone in the IETF is to guarantee the survival of the Internet by ensuring its constant technological change and, in doing so, to ensure its technical excellence. "One has to get consensus through the excellence of the technical work. The search for consensus leads to technical elegance" (Huitema, 1995, p. 24). An important element of the collective identity of Internet engineers is that they see themselves as members of a worldwide elite among network engineers. Affiliation with this elite is defined partly by the ability to avoid pursuing short-term interests of individual organisations and to "serve" the Internet as an overall interest instead. The technical competence of these engineers ensures that persons who violate this ethical code come to attention relatively quickly and lose esteem. The development of interoperable standards, which make the global spread of the Net possible in the first place, is understood as an engine for generating profits with new services or technologies. It is this culturally rooted sense of the common good as an essential resource for profit that facilitates co-operation and determines the way in which dissent and conflicts are dealt with.

All forms of politicking are defiantly rejected in the IETF. The frequently cited example of what the Internet is *not* intended to become is the ISO, whose products bear evidence of strategic horse-trading. Many of the standards developed by the ISO never reach the point of applicability to commercial products and have not been able to prevail over the open Internet standards despite the concerted political backing of ISO member states. In the IETF it is therefore crucial for disputes to be argued on technical grounds only. "In the Internet ... the community attempts to perpetuate the rich tradition and image of 'research and technology first'" (Piscitello and Chapin, 1993, p. 27). If there are competing technical proposals for a solution to a problem, each can be developed by a separate work group to the point of implementation. The fruits of co-operative work are open for objections, critique, and alternative ideas from anyone who wishes to offer them, provided that person is familiar with the preceding discussions. The prerequisite for a new standard to be accepted is the *running code*, that is, at least two independent implementations proving that the technical specification in question functions and that it is interoperable with other technical elements of the Internet (Alvestrand, 1997; RFC 2026, 1996). The market decides which solution eventually wins out.

This arrangement provides the link to the third and final element constituting the Internet model of co-operation, self-restraint. The engineers in the IETF see their task as one of developing technical standards that guarantee the compatibility of commercial products. It is not up to the IETF to decide whether individual standards take hold, so there is great reluctance to deal with questions and issues that go beyond ensuring compatibility and interoperability and enter the territory of industrial product development. The motto is "the market decides", and it holds even for the success of projects to which vast personnel resources have been committed for several years, such as the current effort to develop the next generation of the basic Internet protocol. The fact that the IETF has restricted itself to what is presumably of general commercial interest to a wide range of vendors and users – the technical conditions for the Internet's own survival – may be the key reason why the business community is investing ever-greater human and material resources in this project.

In these ways a new model for the development of international technology and standards has formed around the vision of the Internet (Kowack, 1997; Reidenberg, 1997). It differs from its precursors and from the approach in other fields of technology in two respects. Nation states no longer figure as co-ordinators and mediaries – that role has passed to companies. Those companies had no established models of international co-operative relations to draw on and gradually assumed and transformed the role that the US government research funding had had. A model of centralised organisation, as represented by the telephone companies, is now having to compete against a decentralised form of co-ordination as a key element of the Internet vision and culture defined by binding goals, qualitative criteria and closely circumscribed tasks (Willke, 1997). The rationality of the market-place is supplanting political calculus. Of course, we cannot say what effects these changes will have on the quality of technology, but one can assume that this trend will be repeated in other areas of international co-operation as well. The Internet offers only one piece of evidence that nongovernmental and rather informal, open forms of co-ordination can indeed be successful.

We also find that these different forms of co-operation stipulated by the Internet vision have a recognisable impact on products. The technology of the Net differs substantially from technologies that had previously dominated the communications field. Whereas the companies implementing the vision of national and global "telephony" created a culture and structure of centralisation linked with centralised and proprietary configurations of technology revolving around a single service supplier (the national telephone company) and a single use (telephoning), the Internet's technology reflects a decentralised form of organisation and culture that promotes multiple uses. The more varied the participating industries are, the more flexible and open to multiple applications the resulting technology proves to be. Unlike the triumph of the IBM personal computer or of Microsoft's operating systems DOS and Windows, the rise of a given technical solution to the status of a *de facto* standard is not due to the market clout of a particular company but to the combined competence of all manufacturers. That arrangement may be able to reduce the risk that innovation will be blockaded as it has been in other spheres of economic activity.

At the moment, the Internet is gearing up for what is called real-time uses, such as teleconferencing and other forms of video transmission, with flexible use and open organisational structures the target criteria for future development. Whereas German Telekom, as an outgrowth of the vision and culture of "telephony", is presently going to court to force its competitors to use and pay for its telephone lines and transmission technology, the explicit goal in the Internet is to develop transmission standards that function with all available transmission technologies independently of a specific proprietary status quo, market shares or patents (RFC 1958, 1996). Co-operation among competitors will succeed only if the technology under development is designed to prevent monopolies and ensure equal benefit for all suppliers. All in all, there are many indications that a new model of co-operation and production is emerging, in which technological innovations and organisational learning both require and trigger each other in dynamic reciprocity.

DIFFERING PATTERNS OF INNOVATION: LESSONS TO BE LEARNED

The two innovation strategy case studies of the automotive industry and the Internet reveal heterogeneous trends. Whereas technological development in the automobile industry has a clearly incremental character aimed at preserving the core elements of the automotive society as a vision, telecommunications technology is undergoing major organisational and technological changes that are affecting not only forms of production and co-ordination, but the products themselves. Stagnovation, characterised by the incessant postponement of fundamental modernisation, stands in marked contrast to technological and organisational changes related to paradigm shifts in learning, creating, and supporting bold new technological visions.

The conceptual framework introduced above certainly cannot disclose the substantial causes for the differing innovation patterns found in the automotive and telecommunications sectors. Concepts such as visions, organisational culture and organisational learning draw attention instead to the empirical conditions that may account for the varying *modi operandi* of technological development. More generally, the conceptual framework serves as a means for identifying specific models of technical change and for relating those models to their cultural and organisational environment. In fact, the melding of technical, cultural and organisational aspects can be considered the key element of this conceptual approach. In affording a look at a technical artefact's interplay with broader social perceptions and ideas, organisational traditions and goals, the aim is to avoid both technical and social determinism in explaining technological change.

A comparison of the two case studies brings out differing and similar conditions. For example, both types of innovation are taking place in established markets, even ones highly regulated by public policy. The automotive industry and the institutional structure of the communications industry are both strongly resisting paradigm-shift learning and the emergence of new technological visions. This resistance naturally leads one to ask what it is that has facilitated the advent of a completely new technological vision (the Internet) but left the organisational structures and cultures of the established communications industry relatively unchanged. And in the automotive industry, what is it that has produced neither a new vision nor sweeping changes in existing organisational structures and cultures?

While not able to give an all-encompassing and completely satisfying answer, the two case studies do offer insight into at least some aspects that might explain why certain technological innovations win out and others do not. These aspects are the actors of change as well as the basis for the social and political environment in which they operate. As described above, the Internet was not developed by organisations that had hitherto been responsible for the production of international transmission technology. The transmission protocols of the Internet arose *despite* the resistance of the established telecommunications industry. In other words, the innovation behaviour of the telecommunications companies has not differed fundamentally from that of the automotive industry. The tradition of incremental innovation was broken by the formation of a new constellation of actors and hence the emergence of a new culture of production and development.

This competing model owes its impetus and success not only to the technological superiority of its products but also to the fact that users can choose. Unlike the consumer's options in the automotive industry, which are confined to a few elements and which, in particular, do not include alternatives to the combustion engine, the Internet constitutes a serious alternative to classical written correspondence as well as the telephone. Since this system's success is rooted in the consumer's decisions about use, communication *via* the Internet has in some areas far outpaced telephone communication. The same is true of ongoing technological development of the services on the Internet. The rapid growth of the World Wide Web is due largely to its favourable reception among users. To generalise, user preferences can be an important resource in the acceptance and adoption of profound new technological visions leading to a range of significant technological and organisational innovations. Users are thus to be reckoned as part of the actor constellations that help propagate socially desirable innovations.

Another aspect concerns the social and political environment in which the various innovation strategies are embedded. The decline in the telecommunications companies' power to define further development and regulation in this field of technology is not attributable solely to the success of a competing model; the triumph of the Internet model also reflects a general trend toward deregulation. The disintegration of the traditional monopolistic structure of telecommunications in many western countries fosters the start-up of smaller suppliers who use the existing network either to offer classical services at more favourable rates or, as in the Internet's case, to develop new ways of using the network. Society's interest in new forms of communication and digital services thus coincides with a political willingness to deregulate what was once a public sector. Such conditions are absent in the automotive sector, where there are neither actors with enough influence to offer alternative visions of mobility, nor competing technologies from which a broad stratum of users can choose.

This leads us to the organisational aspects of technical innovation. Two points in particular deserve mentioning. First, the differing innovation patterns exemplified by the automotive and communications industries sharpen the awareness that technical innovation does not automatically lead to organisational innovation, and *vice versa*. Organisational innovations do not spring from new technologies, and the emergence of new organisations is no guarantee that new technologies will be successfully developed and used. Given the breadth and depth of modernism's crisis noted earlier, organisations cannot rely primarily, let alone alternatively, on this or that potential for innovation, hoping that the rest of the necessary innovations will somehow happen on their own sooner or later. In trying to come to grips with the crisis of modernism, the central task of organisations is not to develop technological or organisational potentials for innovation independently of each other, but to meld them systematically. In short, the actual and thus far underdeveloped potential for innovations lies not in technological and organisational innovations *per se*, but in their fusion. That fusion, as it were, represents a second-order potential for innovation. And the ability to perceive and purposefully pursue it is likely to have a large bearing on whether and how much organisations succeed in developing viable strategies for coping with crises.

Second, the two case studies not only alert organisations to the very existence of such second-order potential for innovation, but also make clear why it is possible and necessary for them to focus much more on developing that potential than they have in the past. To be sure, organisations presently have many opportunities to let this potential for innovation lie fallow and to evade the undeniable hardships of developing it. They can do so, for instance, by taking the path of stagnovation and using technological innovations to stabilize and preserve traditional visions, social structures and organisational strategies. The example of Internet standardization shows, however, that such attempts at avoidance can eventually become dead ends. Those dead ends can be reached very quickly, too, particularly when other, usually young and nonestablished organisations combine technological and social innovations and thereby travel down new, unconventional roads. Of course, such forays into unknown terrain are always fraught with risk because it is by no means certain that they will be successful for long if at all. On the other hand, organisations that dare to seek out new chances for growth and development will often come across many opportunities not to be found on the tried and true paths. Today, at the close of the 20th century, where the boundaries of those paths are becoming ever clearer, perhaps the most important task for organisations is to perceive and use such opportunities in order to overcome the crisis of modernism and to be prepared for the challenges of the 21st century.

The stagnovation of the automotive industry and the concurring innovativeness of the telecommunications sector finally raise the question of political lessons that can be drawn from the two case studies. At first glance, the obvious answer seems to be withdrawal of political institutions. Does not the expanding telecommunications sector prove that markets are much more innovative than regulated structures? Unfortunately, the automotive industry seems to exemplify the opposite. Despite growing international competition among private enterprises, fundamental innovations are collectively avoided. Even more striking is that the basic technical innovations in the Internet emerged from public funding. Thus, the relationship between technology development on the one hand and the autonomy of private actors or public regulation on the other turns out to be more complicated than the currently fashionable call for privatisation may suggest. As Schumpeter has argued so convincingly, groundbreaking innovations tend to be a threat to all established norms and institutions, private or public. The unforeseen success of the Internet is a good illustration of this argument. Because no one ever planned to build an open global network to undermine national tariffs and laws, no political body undertook serious efforts to control its development and use. The Internet grew out of a niche, and it took more than twenty years for a broader clientele to begin to discover its benefits. Therefore, one of the lessons to be learned is actually a classic one: the acute financial constraints of many public and private budgets in OECD countries notwithstanding, there is a perpetual reason for allowing for the luxury of niches – to support new ideas and research projects beyond clearly defined short-term goals, both in commercial and academic environments.

NOTES

1. According to RFC 1718 (1994), "The 1st meeting was held in January 1986 at Linkabit in San Diego with 15 attendees. The 4th IETF, held at SRI in Menlo Park in October 1986 was the first at which non-government vendors attended... The 7th IETF, held at MITRE in McLean, Virginia, was the first meeting with over 100 attendees".

2. They are not standards in any formal sense of the term, however. In the language of the Internet, they are called protocols. Their use is open to anyone at no charge and is voluntary. As formulated by one of the engineers working on these protocols: "Voluntary standards have weight in the market place because vendors and users decide to implement and buy products using those standards and choose to attend meetings of those organisations to create those standards. They are fundamentally 'bottom-up' organisations" (J. Day, 2 March 1996, on the "Ipv6 haters" list).

BIBLIOGRAPHY

AKRICH, M. (1992), "Beyond Social Construction of Technology: The Shaping of People and Things in the Innovation Process" in M. Dierkes and U. Hoffmann (eds.), *New Technology at the Outset: Social Forces in the Shaping of Technological Innovations*, Campus, Frankfurt am Main, pp. 173-190.

ALTVATER, E. (1991), *Die Zukunft des Marktes. Ein Essay über die Regulation von Geld und Natur nach dem Scheitern des "real existierenden" Sozialismus*, Westfälisches Dampfboot, Münster.

ALVESTRAND, H.T. (1997), "The Internet Standardisation Process" in T. Buland, H. Finne, S. Helmers, U. Hoffmann and J. Hofmann (eds.), *Management and Network Technology*, European Commission, Brussels, pp. 59-66.

BAECKER, D. (1997), "Weil es so nicht weiter geht: Organisation und Gedächtnis in der Transformationsgesellschaft", *Lettre*, 36(1), pp. 26-29.

BARBEN, D. (1997), "Genese, Enkulturation und Antizipation des Neuen: Über Schwierigkeiten und Nutzen, Leitbilder der Biotechnologie zu re-konstruieren" in M. Dierkes (ed.), *Technikgenese. Befunde aus einem Forschungsprogramm*, Edition Sigma, Berlin, pp. 133-165.

BERTHOIN-ANTAL, A., M. DIERKES and K. HÄHNER (1994), "German Corporate Responsibilities: Statements of Principle", *Journal of General Management*, 19(4), pp. 24-40.

BIJKER, W.E. and J. LAW, eds. (1992), *Shaping Technology, Building Society: Studies in Sociotechnical Change*, MIT, Cambridge, Massachusetts.

BOLTER, J.D. (1990), *Der digitale Faust*, DVA-Oktagon, Stuttgart.

BOYER, R. (1986), "Conclusion: Capitalismes fin de siècle" in R. Boyer (ed.), *Capitalismes fin de siècle*, Presses Universitaires de la France, Paris, pp. 225-244.

BUHR, R. and A. KNIE (1993), "Hätten die mechanischen Schreibmaschinen früher besser sein können?", *Historische Bürowelt*, 35, pp. 11-12.

CALLON, M. (1991), "Techno-Economic Networks and Irreversibility", *Sociological Review Monograph*, 38, pp. 132-161.

CANZLER, W. (1996), *Das Zauberlehrlings-Syndrom. Entstehung und Stabilität des Automobil-Leitbildes*, Edition Sigma, Berlin.

CANZLER, W., S. HELMERS and U. HOFFMANN (1995), *Die Datenautobahn – Sinn und Unsinn einer populären Metapher*, WZB Discussion Paper FS II 95-101, Wissenschaftszentrum Berlin für Sozialforschung.

CANZLER, W. and A. KNIE (1994), *Das Ende des Automobils – Fakten und Trends zum Umbau der Autogesellschaft*, C.F. Müller, Heidelberg.

CANZLER, W. and L. MARZ (1997), "Stagnovation: Der Automobilpakt und die gedopte Arbeitsgesellschaft", *Universitas*, 610, pp. 359-371.

CERF, V. (1993), "How the Internet Came To Be" in B. Aboba (ed.), *The Online User's Encyclopedia*, Addison-Wesley, Reading.

COMER, D.E. (1991), *Internetworking with TCP/IP. Vol I. – Principles, Protocols, and Architecture*, Prentice-Hall, Englewood Cliffs, New Jersey.

COY, W. (1994), "Gutenberg und Turing: Fünf Thesen zur Geburt der Hypermedien", *Zeitschrift für Semiotik*, 1-2, pp. 69-74.

CROCKER, D. (1993), "Making Standards the IETF Way", *Standard View*, 1(1).

DERRIDA, J. (1996), *Marx' Gespenster: Der Staat der Schuld, die Trauerarbeit und die neue Internationale*, Suhrkamp, Frankfurt am Main.

DIERKES, M. (1985), "Research in Search of Relevance and Excellence: The Management of Creativity in the Social Sciences" in Robert Lawrence Kuhn (ed.), *Frontiers in Creative and Innovative Management*, Ballinger Publishing Company, Cambridge, Massachusetts, pp. 221-243.

DIERKES, M. (1988), "Unternehmenskultur und Unternehmensführung", *Zeitschrift für Betriebswirtschaft*, 5/6, pp. 554-575.

DIERKES, M. (1990), "Technische Entwicklung als sozialer Prozeß: Chancen und Grenzen einer sozialwissenschaftlichen Erklärung der Technikgenese", *Naturwissenschaften*, 5/90.

DIERKES, M. (1992), "Leitbild, Lernen und Unternehmensentwicklung: Wie können Unternehmen sich vorausschauend veränderten Umfeldbedingungen stellen?" in C. Krebsbach-Gnath (ed.), *Den Wandel in Unternehmen steuern: Faktoren für ein erfolgreiches Change-Management*, Frankfurter Allgemeine Zeitung, Frankfurt am Main, pp. 19-36.

DIERKES, M. (1993), *Die Technisierung und ihre Folgen: Zur Biographie eines Forschungsfeldes*, Edition Sigma, Berlin.

DIERKES, M. (1994), "Leitbilder der Technik – ihre Bedeutungen, Funktionen und Potentiale für den KI-Diskurs" in Verein Deutscher Ingenieure (VDI) (ed.), *VDI-Report 21: Künstliche Intelligenz – Leitvorstellungen und Verantwortbarkeit*, Vol. 2, VDI, Düsseldorf, pp. 83-98.

DIERKES, M. (1997), "Zukunftswissenschaft? Über den Ausgangspunkt und die (Un-) Realisierbarkeit einer Forschungsanforderung", *Wechselwirkung*, 83, pp. 46-56.

DIERKES, M., R. BUHR, W. CANZLER and A. KNIE (1995), *Erosionen des Automobil-Leitbildes: Auflösungserscheinungen, Beharrungstendenzen, neue technische Optionen und Aushandlungsprozesse einer zukünftigen Mobilitätspolitik. Begründung eines Forschungsvorhabens*, WZB Discussion Paper FS II 95-107, Wissenschaftszentrum Berlin für Sozialforschung.

DIERKES, M., W. CANZLER, L. MARZ and A. KNIE (1995), "Politik und Technikgenese", *Verbund Sozialwissenschaftliche Technikforschung. Mitteilungen*, 15, pp. 7-28.

DIERKES, M. and K. HÄHNER (1994), "Unternehmenslernen als Komponente des Wachstums", in H. Albach (ed.), *Globale soziale Marktwirtschaft: Ziele-Wege-Akteure*, Gabler, Wiesbaden, pp. 247-262.

DIERKES, M., K. HÄHNER and A. BERTHOIN-ANTAL (1997), *Das Unternehmen und sein Umfeld. Wahrnehmungsprozesse und Unternehmenskultur am Beispiel eines Chemiekonzerns*, Campus, Frankfurt am Main.

DIERKES, M. and U. HOFFMANN, eds. (1992), *New Technology at the Outset: Social Forces in the Shaping of Technological Innovations*, Campus, Frankfurt am Main.

DIERKES, M., U. HOFFMANN and L. MARZ (1996), *Visions of Technology: Social and Institutional Factors Shaping the Development of New Technologies*, St. Martins, New York.

DIERKES, M. and L. MARZ (1994), "Unternehmensverantwortung und leitbildorientierte Technikgestaltung" in W. Zimmerli and V. Brennecke (eds.), *Technikverantwortung in der Unternehmenskultur. Von theoretischen Konzepten zur praktischen Umsetzung*, Schäffer-Poeschel, Stuttgart, pp. 89-114.

DIERKES, M. and L. MARZ. (1998), *Leitbild und Lernen: Zum Organisationslernen in Krisen* (Manuscript in preparation).

DIERKES, M. and K. ZIMMERMANN, eds. (1996), *Sozialstaat in der Krise. Hat die soziale Marktwirtschaft noch eine Chance?*, Gabler, Wiesbaden.

FOURASTIÉ, J. (1979), *Les trentes glorieuses ou la révolution invisible de 1946 à 1975*, Fayard, Paris.

FUKUYAMA, F. (1992), *Das Ende der Geschichte. Wo stehen wir?*, Kindler, Munich.

GENSCHEL, P. (1995), *Standards in der Informationstechnik. Institutioneller Wandel in der internationalen Standardisierung*, Campus, Frankfurt am Main.

GLYN, A., A. HUGHES, A. LIPIETZ, and A. SINGH (1990), "The Rise and Fall of the Golden Age" in S. Marglin and J.B. Schor (eds.), *The Golden Age of Capitalism: Reinterpreting the Postwar Experience*, Clarendon, Oxford, pp. 39-125.

GRASSMUCK, V. (1995), "Die Turing-Galaxis: Das Universal-Medium auf dem Weg zur Weltsimulation", *Lettre International*, I, pp. 48-55.

GROTE, C. v., S. HELMERS, U. HOFFMANN and J. HOFMANN, eds. (1994), *Kommunikationsnetze der Zukunft – Leitbilder und Praxis*, WZB Discussion Paper FS II 94-103, Wissenschaftszentrum Berlin für Sozialforschung.

HAFNER, K. and M. LYON (1996), *Where Wizards Stay Up Late: The Origins of the Internet*, Simon and Schuster, New York.

HELLIGE, H.D. (ed.), *Technikleitbilder auf dem Prüfstand. Leitbild-Assessment aus Sicht der Informatik- und Computergeschichte*, Edition Sigma, Berlin.

HELMERS, S., U. HOFFMANN and J. HOFMANN (1996a), *Netzkultur und Netzwerkorganisation. Das Projekt "Interaktionsraum Internet"*, WZB Discussion Paper FS II 96-103, Wissenschaftszentrum Berlin für Sozialforschung.

HELMERS, S., U. HOFFMANN and J. HOFMANN (1996b), "Standard Development as Techno-social Ordering: The Case of the Next Generation of the Internet Protocol" in

T. Buland, H. Finne, S. Helmers, U. Hoffmann and J. Hofmann (eds.), *Mangement and Network Technology*, European Commission, Brussels, pp. 35-58.

HOFFMANN, U. and L. MARZ (1992), "Leitbildperspektiven. Technische Innovationen zwischen Vorstellung und Verwirklichung" in K. Burmeister and K. Steinmüller (eds.), *Streifzüge ins Übermorgen. Science Fiction und Zukunftsforschung*, Beltz, Weinheim, pp. 197-222.

HOFMANN, J. (1996), "Vorstellungen und Bilder in der Technikerzeugung – Eine Episode aus der Biographie des schreibenden Computers" in H.D. Hellige (ed.), *Technikleitbilder auf dem Prüfstand: Leitbild-Assessment aus Sicht der Informatik – und Computergeschichte*, Edition Sigma, Berlin, pp. 161-184.

HOFMANN, J. (1997), "Über Nutzerbilder in Textverarbeitungsprogrammen – Drei Fallbeispiele" in M. Dierkes (ed.), *Technikgenese. Befunde aus einem Forschungsprogramm*, Edition Sigma, Berlin, pp. 71-97.

HUITEMA, C. (1995), *Routing in the Internet*, Prentice-Hall, Englewood Cliffs, New Jersey.

JASANOFF, S., ed. (1995), *Handbook of Science and Technology Studies*, Sage, Thousand Oaks, California.

JOERGES, B. (1993), *Große technische Systeme. Zum Problem technischer Größenordnung und Maßstäblichkeit*, WZB Discussion Paper FS II 93-507, Wissenschaftszentrum Berlin für Sozialforschung.

KNIE, A. (1994), *Wankel-Mut in der Automobil-Industrie. Anfang und Ende einer Antriebsalternative*, Edition Sigma, Berlin.

KNIE, A., ed. (1997), *Die Neuerfindung urbaner Automobilität: Elektroautos in den USA und in Europa* (Manuscript in preparation).

KOWACK, G. (1997), Internet Governance and the Emergence of Global Civil Society, *IEEE Communications Magazine*, 35(5), pp. 52-57.

KRUPP, C. (1995), *Klimaänderung und die Folgen. Eine exemplarische Fallstudie über die Möglichkeiten und Grenzen einer interdisziplinären Klimafolgenforschung*, Edition Sigma, Berlin.

LA PORTE, T. (1991), *Social Responses to Large Technical Systems: Control and Anticipation*, Kluwer, Dordrecht.

LATOUR, B. (1995), *Wir sind nie modern gewesen. Versuch einer symmetrischen Anthropologie*, Akademie Verlag, Berlin.

LAW, J. (1992), Notes on the Theory of the Actor-Network: Ordering, Strategy, and Heterogeneity", *Systems Practice*, 5, pp. 379-393.

LEHR, W. (1995), "Compatibility Standards and Interoperability: Lessons from the Internet" in B. Kahin and J. Abbate (eds.), *Standards Policy for Information Infrastructure*, MIT, Cambridge, Massachusetts, pp. 121-147.

MARZ, L. (1993a), *Leitbild und Diskurs: Eine Fallstudie zur diskursiven Technikfolgenabschätzung von Informationstechniken*, WZB Discussion Paper FS II 93-106, Wissenschaftszentrum Berlin für Sozialforschung.

MARZ, L. (1993b), *Das Leitbild der posthumanen Vernunft. Zur diskursiven Technikfolgenabschätzung der "Künstlichen Intelligenz"*, WZB Discussion Paper FS II 93-111, Wissenschaftszentrum Berlin für Sozialforschung.

MARZ, L. and M. DIERKES (1994), "Leitbildprägung und Leitbildgestaltung: Zum Beitrag der Technikgenese-Forschung für eine prospektive Technikfolgen-Regulierung" in G. Bechmann and T. Petermann (eds.), *Interdisziplinäre Technikforschung: Genese, Folgen, Diskurs*, Campus, Frankfurt am Main, pp. 35-71.

MAYNTZ, R. (1993), "Große technische Systeme und ihre gesellschaftstheoretische Bedeutung", *Kölner Zeitschrift für Soziologie und Sozialpsychologie*, 45(1), pp. 97-108.

MORAVEC, H. (1990), *Mind Children: Der Wettlauf zwischen menschlicher und künstlicher Intelligenz*, Hoffmann and Campe, Hamburg.

NRC (National Research Council), ed. (1988), *The Behavioral and Social Sciences: Achievements and Opportunities*, National Academy Press, Washington, DC.

OFFE, C. (1984), *"Arbeitsgesellschaft": Strukturprobleme und Zukunftsperspektiven*, Campus, Frankfurt am Main.

PAWLOWSKY, P. (1994), *Wissensmanagement in der lernenden Organisation*, Postdoctoral Dissertation, University of Paderborn.

PISCITELLO, David M. and A.L. CHAPIN (1993), *Open Systems Networking: TCP/IP and OSI*, Addsion-Wesley, Reading.

REIDENBERG, J.R. (1997), "Governing Networks and Rule-making in Cyberspace" in B. Kahin and C. Nesson, *Borders in Cyberspace*, MIT, Cambridge, Massachusetts, pp. 84-105.

RFC 1000: J. Postel and J. Reynolds (1987), *Request For Comments Reference Guide*.

RFC 1718: The IETF Secretariat and G. Malkin (1994), *The Tao of IETF – A Guide for New Attendees of the Internet Engineering Task Force*.

RFC 1958: B. Carpenter (1996), *Architectural Principles of the Internet*.

RFC 2026: S. Bradner (1996), *The Internet Standards Process – Revision 3*.

RHEINGOLD, H. (1992), *Virtuelle Welten. Reisen im Cyberspace*, Rowohlt, Reinbek.

ROGERS, R.A. (1990), *Visions Dancing in Engineers' Heads: AT&T's Quest to Fullfill the Leitbild of a Universal Telephone Service*, WZB Discussion Paper FS II 90-102, Wissenschaftszentrum Berlin für Sozialforschung.

SALUS, P.H. (1995), *Casting the Net: From Arpanet to Internet and Beyond*, Addison-Wesley, Reading, Massachusetts.

WAGNER, P. (1995), *Soziologie der Moderne: Freiheit und Disziplin*, Campus, Frankfurt am Main.

WILLKE, H. (1997), "Informationstechnische Vernetzung als Infrastrukturaufgabe – Welche Rolle spielt die Politik?" in R. Werle and C. Lang (eds.), *Modell Internet? Entwicklungsperspektiven neuer Kommunikationsnetze*, Campus, Frankfurt am Main, pp. 115-132.

6

ENABLING MACRO CONDITIONS FOR REALISING TECHNOLOGY'S POTENTIAL

by

Emilio Fontela
University Autonoma of Madrid, Spain

INTRODUCTION: TECHNOLOGY AND LONG-TERM ECONOMIC TRENDS

Economists interested in long-term trends often identify different periods of the 19th and 20th centuries during which clusters of innovations were introduced on a massive scale. These innovations were developed in specific geographical areas with distinct socio-cultural and economic characteristics (mainly in Western Europe and the United States), and were later diffused progressively and selectively to the rest of the world.[1]

At the end of the 20th century, we are witnessing similar processes taking place in a wider area (OECD Member countries) with a new cluster of technologies mainly relating to microelectronics, to computers and telecommunications (the Information Society Technologies), and to biotechnologies, new energy sources and new materials.

Of course, many of the past, present and future innovations derive strictly from increased scientific and technological knowledge, but it is also evident that the selection of these innovations and the extent of their success depends heavily on the socio-economic context. Technological development, in its final innovative outcomes, is both supply-pushed (by scientific knowledge) and demand-pulled (by social and economic needs).

At the threshold of the 21st century, the OECD economies are witnessing unprecedented changes:

- Internally they are rediscovering the need for more active market mechanisms, especially in the services area (deregulation and privatisation of transport and telecommunications, liberalisation of financial services, etc.).
- Externally they are facing the deep shift of the rest of the world from centralised planning to increasingly market-driven economic systems (over

3 billion people have moved in this direction in recent years), thereby creating new business opportunities but also bringing new competitive players into their traditional markets.

Despite the obvious dynamism of this process of market broadening, the overall macroeconomic performance of the OECD countries is falling short of expectations. The GDP growth rate remains low, and unemployment (especially in Europe) has reached socially unacceptable levels. Following the postwar recovery period and the subsequent economic boom, the advanced industrialised countries have apparently lost momentum.

Furthermore, the rate of change of total factor productivity (TFP), which measures the macroeconomic gains from productive innovations,[2] has often decreased, which is quite puzzling. Are the new technologies proving unable to increase the overall efficiency of the economic system?

Economic researchers have devoted considerable attention to technological innovation, and some relations have been reasonably well established, both theoretically and empirically.

The following two sections extract from this existing body of knowledge what appear to be the longer-term aspects of the relationship between technology and the economy. These observations should help to set the boundaries for scenarios to 2020/2030, which are then developed. The chapter concludes with an attempt to envisage the main macroeconomic aspects of the coming Information Society.

SOME SOCIO-ECONOMIC ASPECTS OF TECHNICAL CHANGES

The relatively benign neglect of the analysis of technical change by modern neoclassical macroeconomic literature has been compensated by extensive empirical analysis of the aggregate production function and of TFP as the intangible component of output (or value-added) growth (in neoclassical frameworks, with perfect competition and constant returns to scale, TFP measures shifts in the production functions that are to be interpreted as technical change).

Recent research by the OECD on growth accounting during the 1970s and 1980s estimates the average annual rate of GDP growth (for a sample of ten Member countries) at 2.9 per cent for the twenty-year period, with contributions by labour increasing at a rate of 0.6 per cent, those by capital at a rate of 1.1 per cent and the remaining 1.2 per cent deriving from TFP growth (therefore, roughly 40 per cent of total growth is explained by TFP).[3]

What exactly is the source of these TFP gains? Of course it is technical change, but understood in a very broad sense. Whereas the explanation of TFP change may be empirically related to technological development variables like R&D or to human resources variables such as the educational level of the labour force[4] (and there is abundant proof of both), a more comprehensive understanding of the process at work is required. Reference could be made to modern management theories, in which the competitiveness of the firm basically hinges on:

– technological capabilities;
– human capabilities;
– organisational capabilities.[5]

At a macro level, we could similarly assume that TFP growth is the result of an accumulation process of intangible (technological, human and organisational) capital. This intangible capital is mostly complementary to tangible capital and is probably a substitute for labour (a country such as the United States with relatively low TFP growth also exhibits a relatively low growth rate in labour productivity; Europe, with relatively high TFP growth rates, faces serious unemployment problems). In general, there is no expansion without tangible investment and no innovation without intangible investment.[6]

While it is obvious that there is a direct link between technological accumulation and R&D spending, and between human resources accumulation and educational investments, the accumulation of organisational capabilities is more opaque and includes notions like the efficiency of infrastructures,[7] the functioning of institutions and of the regulatory framework, and – most likely – a vast array of cultural elements.[8] Needless to say, it also includes the changing characteristics of the productive structure itself – of the overall organisation of production in interrelated commodities and industries.

In this context, among the more recent contributions to the analysis of technical change in the OECD countries, two aspects provide insights of particular interest for the analysis of possible future developments:

– technological spillovers; and
– the institutional matching of innovations.

Technological spillovers

The interdependent aspects of the production structure induce externalities associated with innovations, usually called "knowledge spillovers" when they refer to the use of technological knowledge developed in one industry by another industry, or "rent spillovers" when they refer to a price decrease or quality improvement of inputs supplied by an innovating industry to its clients.

That knowledge spillovers indeed exist is clear from patent data and from data from innovation surveys: any economic sector relies for its development on technological developments emanating from other sectors. Several studies have also shown that the R&D efforts of supplier industries (appropriately weighted with technical input-output coefficients) partly explain the TFP growth of the client industry.

As R&D is only one aspect of the technological accumulation process, and as the latter is also only a part of the total accumulation of intangible capital, one should expect an industry's TFP growth to be even better explained by a weighted combination of the TFP growth of the supplier industries.[9]

It is thus clear that the structure of an economy is an important component of its TFP growth, and therefore of its innovative capacity.

When considering "rent spillovers", other issues come into focus. The idea behind rent spillovers is that, as a result of an innovation, a supplier may either decrease its price or increase its quality, thus helping the client to increase its own TFP. This raises the question of the appropriation of TFP gains, and directly refers to the market structure. Perfect competition will lead to decreasing prices (or increasing quality) by the innovator, while a monopolist will be able to take full advantage of the rent generated by innovation.[10]

Rent spillovers are an important component of growth processes in advanced industrial countries: decreases in relative prices of manufactured products resulting from TFP growth induce demand elasticity reactions that stimulate output growth and further increases of TFP. Such a virtuous circle fundamentally supported the growth process of the 1950s and 1960s, and was substantially eroded in the 1970s and 1980s (with increasing saturation of consumer durables changing the elasticity reactions, and with more constraints encountered in the innovative processes of many manufacturing industries, especially at the level of intermediate and basic goods).[11]

Matching technological and socio-economic change

Neo-Schumpeterian analysis of the long waves of economic development and their relationship with changes in the technological paradigms has further elaborated the argument that depressions are the consequence of a mismatch between a new technological system and the evolution of surrounding social, economic or institutional systems.[12]

For its full development, a new technological paradigm (interpreted as a coincident cluster of basic innovations) cannot be dissociated from new productive organisation, new income distributions, new employment structures, new consumption patterns, new relations between public and private activities, etc. Thus, the new technologies of the Information Society are a source of problems for the old socio-economic structures, and they cannot develop their entire positive potential until society and social institutions are able to match perfectly with them.

During a transition period such as the one that we are witnessing at the end of the 20th century, the new socio-economic systems that will achieve the technological potential of the Information Society are still at an embryonic stage, and many alternative scenarios remain open for the future.

TECHNOLOGICAL CHANGE, ECONOMIC GROWTH AND EMPLOYMENT

The previous section pointed out that successful realisation of technology's potential at the macro level will depend not only on concrete efforts in R&D and education, but also on the economic system structure (its capacity for inducing spillovers of knowledge and rent) and on its matching the rest of the social systems. This section examines the effect that the realisation of this technology's potential may have upon the economic and social structure.

An important insight into the issue is provided by Baumol's model of unbalanced growth;[13] if some sectors of an economy show rapidly growing TFP as a result of increased innovative activities while others remain more or less stagnant in terms of technological change, the relative prices of the output of the stagnant sectors will progressively increase, and workers will move to these stagnant sectors.

A real understanding of the frontier between sectors with progressive or stagnant TFP growth has to do with Baumol's differentiation of the role of labour: when labour is primarily an instrument ("an incidental requisite for the attainment of the final product"), it can be progressively replaced by other instruments, but that is simply impossible when "labour is itself the end-product". Of course many service activities have human labour as an end-product and their TFP should be relatively stagnant; however, practically all manufacturing activities and many services (in particular the network services of transportation, communication or finance) have end-products that do not necessarily require human labour. Thus, in the very long run, Baumol's model points to a social redefinition of the role of work and employment, and the speed of this change will be a function of the speed of introduction of new labour-saving technologies by the sectors with high TFP.

Despite its simple dichotomy, the unbalanced growth model provides quite a good explanation of some fundamental macroeconomic processes of change in the advanced industrial societies in recent decades. Some service sectors have been growing in employment and in relative prices, while their total share of real output has remained relatively constant; this structural transformation may partly explain the overall loss of momentum by economic growth.[14]

Assuming that the sectors where innovations occur can, through price decreases (or quality improvements), transmit some (or all) of the gains to the users, the final growth outcome will depend on final demand, either directly (if the innovations are at consumer level) or indirectly (if they relate to intermediate products or to capital goods). Thus the price and income elasticities of demand play an essential role in establishing the dynamic response to innovative change.

If it is further assumed that, in the OECD Member countries, many manufactured goods are close to saturation levels (and are thus increasingly less elastic in response to income or price changes), the key question concerns the possibility for the new technologies either to develop entirely new manufactured products corresponding to new consumption functions (e.g. the PC), or to lower the prices of some services and find adequate elastic demands in those cases. While there may be intrinsic limitations to the continuous development of new manufactured products, the case for services seems rather clear since, for many of them, saturation is difficult to envisage (e.g. education, health, leisure, transportation, communication or information services).

Under these assumptions, the future growth model of the OECD countries greatly depends on the introduction of new technologies into service sectors that are still using instrumental labour. (These are the only ones in which technological innovation is possible since, by definition, sectors where labour is the product cannot be technologically changed – although they could be technologically replaced and/or their qualitative content technologically modified.)

SCENARIOS

When facing the problem of the introduction of new technologies, the advanced industrial countries of the OECD have to consider a number of challenging issues; the following require special attention:

- Will it be possible to maintain a high level of welfare and employment?
- Will it be possible to sustain ecological balances?
- How will the new technological developments affect relations with the rest of the world?

These challenges really question the growth model associated with the new technologies – the growth model of the Information Society. The characteristics of this model can be explored by examining alternative scenarios – and these in turn can offer insights into the most likely future alternative paths.

The first scenario ("Conventional Wisdom") reflects the present set of opinions about the future (which normally reflect the recent past as well as some clearly identified long-term trends).

To further deepen the analysis, two alternative scenarios centred on opposite views about the role of government in promoting innovation policies will be considered. These alternatives are simple transformations of the Conventional Wisdom scenario; the first reinforces the transfer of responsibilities to market mechanisms (the "Market" scenario), and the second reinforces the institutional processes (the "New Society" scenario).

The analysis is thus constructed around a central path, which is greatly dependent on supposedly realistic present situations, surrounded by a band which is limited by "pure" radical concepts with low probability of occurrence (as real systems tend to be complex and more "mixed"). If the Conventional Wisdom scenario is correctly oriented, the band should encompass cyclical fluctuations around this central path, *i.e.* fluctuations between socio-political contexts that are characteristic of modern advanced industrial societies.

The Conventional Wisdom scenario

Efforts to elaborate coherent long-term pictures of large economic and social systems are rather infrequent, although the number of partial long-term studies on specific issues is increasing.[15]

Some of the more relevant features of the Conventional Wisdom scenario could be the following:

– The world, and especially the OECD area, is expected to strengthen economic integration processes, with the EU successfully developing the EMU, and with the creation of large free-trade areas (in the Pacific basin, in the Americas, and possibly in the Atlantic zone), within a general trend towards the elimination of all trade and non-trade barriers (WTO).

– Services sectors, which traditionally operated in overregulated and overprotected national markets, will be open to competition; this trend, already evident in key service sectors such as finance, transportation and communication, is expected to reduce the "sheltered" areas of national economies only to the permanently shrinking public service activities; social services traditionally delivered in monopolistic conditions by public agents are increasingly expected to be open to competitive supply by private agents (contestable markets).

– The expected greater international competition in all markets for products and services should stimulate globalisation processes with regard to economic production agents (large multinational firms or networks of firms based on agreements about technology, production facilities, marketing, etc.); these processes of globalisation are already evident in the financial services sector, but they are also developing rapidly in manufacturing (*e.g.* automobiles) and other services (*e.g.* telecommunications).

– Access to technology and to finance are considered necessary factors for competitiveness at all levels (firms and even regions and nations); in the

OECD countries, continuous investments in R&D should solidly establish scientific and technological world leadership.

To summarise these main features of a Conventional Wisdom scenario for the first decades of the 21st century, it can be said that this period is expected to be characterised by the emergence of a "global economic system" increasingly oriented by both a technological and an economic logic of competitiveness and efficiency. The new system has clear agents (the firms), but the role of the state needs some redefinition.

This Conventional Wisdom scenario refers to often implicit views about the future that are considered to be most likely by long-term analysts. Among these views, the following address the challenging issues mentioned above with special reference to the OECD area.

a) Growth and employment

It is generally felt that, despite the innovation activity associated with the new technologies (IT, biotechnologies, new materials) and the productivity gains to be expected from increased trade specialisation (resulting from the elimination of international trade barriers) and from the efficiency of financial globalisation (lowering overall transaction costs for the world economy), the growth rate of the OECD countries will remain relatively low, in terms of both population and economic activity (see Table 1).

Table 1. **Population and GDP growth rates (PPP)**

(annual rates, in percentage)

	Population		GDP (PPP)	
	1995/1960	2030/1995	1995/1960	2030/1995
World	1.8	1.1	3.7	3.8
OECD	0.9	0.3	3.3	2.1

Source: CEPII, 1996.[16]

As a result of this process, the OECD economies, which accounted for 59 per cent of world output in 1960 and 52 per cent in 1995, are expected to account for less than 30 per cent of world output in 2030. There is, however, little doubt that the OECD area, as the most technologically advanced region of the world, will continue to be the main source of new technological developments and innovation.

The new technologies are expected to change practically all products, processes and lifestyles and the organisation of production, distribution and consumption, as well as the functioning of the financial system. Conventional Wisdom directly associates new technologies with the development of competitiveness in firms, regions and nations, thus justifying active public policies in this area. Increasing world security, implying a relative decrease of defence-related technological research, is expected to reorient R&D efforts towards economic and social goals.[17]

It is also generally agreed that the decades ahead will confirm the progressive move towards a "global" economy, with complete freedom of movement for goods and services. In this framework, manufacturing activities are also expected to develop relatively faster outside the OECD area. Thus, in the Conventional Wisdom scenario there remain serious doubts as to how full employment could be achieved in the OECD countries. A shift towards greater employment in tertiary activities is often contemplated as a possibility, but there are a number of services sectors, mainly the "network" services (such as energy distribution, transport, communications, trade, finance and banking, insurance and real estate), that are already showing signs of a declining workforce.[18] Employment creation is therefore expected to concentrate on the knowledge production and personal services sectors (management, research, healthcare, education, leisure, government, and even housekeeping) or in the "change sector" (innovation development activities in all sectors), mainly for "brain-workers" for whom labour is the final product and, alternatively, for "low-level service workers" (still performing activities that do not justify capital investment for automation).

The concept of "labour as a product" creates great differences in the income-generating capacity of the workers, which will fundamentally depend on the market value of these "products" – itself a function of cultural backgrounds. Increased income inequality is therefore associated implicitly with the Conventional Wisdom growth model, and several options remain open for government policies. (At present, the United States accepts the unequal income distribution effect; most European countries implicitly prefer income redistribution and unemployment; and Japan culturally values some low-productivity service work more highly and, therefore, operates with wider differences in relative prices.)

b) Quality of life and the environment

The conventional view about the long-term future of environmental quality considers the growing importance of problems of a global, regional or urban nature, and the need for active policies (taxes and regulations, or public expenditure). In general, great expectations are placed on the successful introduction of new technologies (for improving quality of life, for clean production processes, for re-establishing ecological balancing processes, etc.) that, again, require active public R&D policies.

The long-term "desirable image" of ecologically sustainable economic growth in the OECD therefore requires public policies with priority levels that will differ widely among countries. However, the Conventional Wisdom scenario remains relatively optimistic: in the framework of growth and technological development outlined in a) above, the OECD economies should be able to greatly improve their ecological sustainability and quality of life during the coming decades.

c) Relations with the rest of the world

The Conventional Wisdom scenario assumes that the rest of the world will continuously move towards economic and social systems aligned with those adopted traditionally by OECD countries, thus that they will rely largely on markets and on democratically controlled governments enacting policies compatible with market functioning.

This aspect of the Conventional Wisdom scenario is currently supported in the IMF policy recommendations, in the WTO actions, and in the trend towards globalisation within the financial system (enhanced by the technological diffusion of computing and telecommunications).

In this context, the OECD area is expected to act as a technological centre, using its innovative gains to maintain both a competitive trade position and leadership in technology transfers and FDI. In general, while accepting the OECD countries' relative decline in importance in the world economy, the Conventional Wisdom scenario is fundamentally optimistic as to their technology-based growth model. After the end of the cold war, the advanced industrialised countries expect a period of greater economic stability and development worldwide; Conventional Wisdom envisages a set of powerful developments that are likely to strengthen the OECD economies' position: their leadership in the development of new technologies and in financial markets. Finance and technology are the winning factors for competitiveness, and in both of them the OECD area enjoys a clear advantage over the rest of the world. That Conventional Wisdom does not expect this advantage to translate into higher growth and employment in the OECD countries in the 21st century shows that there are other socio-political constraints (mainly dealing with demography, values or institutions) affecting this economic scenario.

The Market scenario

The Market scenario is envisaged as a sideline of the Conventional Wisdom scenario that strongly emphasizes the more extreme extant proposals for the application of perfect market economics.[19] It is therefore based on the same general ideas concerning the future of free trade in goods and services and the globalisation of economic markets and agents. The main difference with respect to the Conventional Wisdom scenario lies in the definition of the frontier between market and non-market activities. In the Market scenario, the activities of public entities are reduced to those of a "minimal" state (justice, defence and administration); regulation by the democratically elected government of the state replaces direct public intervention. The state ceases entirely to be a producer of services of direct economic relevance (transport, communications) and transfers the production of social services (education, health, insurance, etc.) to the private sector.

In the area of science and technology, the state also avoids any activity of potential economic relevance (which must therefore be developed by private economic agents). As a consequence of the privatisation of traditional public services, firms active in these markets are expected to follow the logic of globalisation, thus widening their area of influence beyond national frontiers.

a)   Growth and employment

Should the OECD be able to follow the path of a Market scenario, there are reasons to believe that the growth rate of production could be higher than in the Conventional Wisdom scenario:

- The transfer of social services to market forces should, in principle, stimulate their rate of innovation under competitive pressure; the new IT, applied in education and in healthcare, could reach higher levels of diffusion.

- Facing price- and income-elastic demands, fully privatised social services could contribute to a "virtuous" circle of demand – further production – relative price declines – further demand.

- The minimal state should be able to reduce the tax burden and to eliminate budget deficits, thus allowing for lower capital costs for private investments.

Because the new technological wave is centred on IT, and because these technologies are particularly relevant in the services area, it would seem that the positive expected impacts of their introduction will depend greatly upon the innovative dynamism of services, and it is generally accepted that this dynamism is greater in market conditions: the liberalisation of capital markets has already greatly stimulated financial innovation and financial efficiency, and has been linked to a process of rapid technological change and globalisation. The same applies to other key sectors of the economy, such as telecommunications and air transport, that have been stimulated technologically and strategically by deregulation and privatisation processes in many OECD countries.

IT's accelerated introduction in the services sector (especially in the social services) should greatly modify the demand for labour; as already seen in agriculture and in most manufacturing, instrumental labour should also progressively disappear rapidly in many services activities (thus intensifying the evolution towards a "labour as product" situation), particularly in the traditional network services (*e.g.* transportation or finance) but also in "new" network services in education and healthcare by making extensive use of information technologies. The weight of the employment issue therefore increases in this scenario.

In a pure Market scenario, however, full employment is obtained directly in a flexible labour market without regulatory constraints (such as a minimum wage) or oligopolistic positions, simply by a real decrease in the average wage rate.

Needless to say, the main negative results under this scenario relate to income distribution: we could expect rapid growth of inequality to socially unacceptable levels, as already observed in the recent past in countries that have moved in the direction of the "minimal state" (*e.g.* Argentina) or deep deregulation (*e.g.* the United States).

In the area of technology and innovation, market failures might lower the expected economic growth.

First, it is possible that the low probability of appropriation of research results in basic science might lead to under-investment in this field, thus reducing the flow of supply-pushed new technologies. Secondly, it is also possible that competition in advanced technology areas might induce over-investment in applied research. The overall balance of the R&D output may not reach the market's initial optimal expectations.

b) Quality of life and the environment

It is difficult to associate high levels of quality of life with very unequal income distributions. Furthermore, it is difficult for pure markets (which operate with myopic short-term objectives) to correctly handle environmental problems. Thus, in terms of quality of life and the environment, the Market scenario would rank below the Conventional Wisdom scenario.

c) Relations with the rest of the world

In the context of a Market scenario, the OECD countries would limit co-operation policies with the rest of the world to those of "mutual interest". In a purely competitive situation one could expect some the poorest countries to break with the system – and again, there would be a widening gap between rich and poor countries.

From the point of view of technology transfer, this scenario points to a progressive extension of the OECD zone; the rest of the world would subsequently develop competitive economic systems compatible with the technologies of the OECD countries.

Modern telecommunications and transport infrastructures, which contribute to a reduction of economic transaction costs and (thus) to a reduction of geographical distance, should play an essential role in this context. Since, in a Market scenario, infrastructure would basically be developed by private capital at market rates of return, this development should essentially follow potential demand, an evolution that clearly points in the direction of building on existing links rather than designing entirely new ones.

In general, the Market scenario is a scenario of economic efficiency, with Darwinian selection processes acting at the level of individuals, as well as of institutions or even nations. This process always risks leaving many casualties behind, and the economic welfare gains may not compensate for the social welfare losses. In terms of technological developments and innovations, the Market scenario (which should, in principle, stimulate the path of change) might well end up creating supply constraints and short-termism, as a result of wrong investment decisions (market failures).

The New Society scenario

The New Society scenario is also envisaged as a sideline of the Conventional Wisdom scenario that strongly emphasizes the more extreme extant proposals for social control of technology.[20] In this scenario, technological public policies are essentially redirected from assisting competitive economic processes, to the more direct satisfaction of social needs.

Rather than moving in the minimal direction, the state in this scenario – which envisages entirely new ways of functioning for social structures (changing the relations between education, work and leisure in particular) – expands both its regulatory activity and its direct service production.

The general framework of the other two scenarios (free trade in goods and services, globalisation of economic agents) is kept constant, but the New Society concept is developed by the different nations, with alternative features including:

- A new Welfare State oriented towards the collective needs of a society in which "instrumental" work has practically disappeared and all work is therefore more of the "labour as product" type (vocational, self-promoted, permanently changing). The state is expected in this context to provide equal opportunities for self-realisation and corresponding safety nets (in a productive system in which all producers cannot "deliver" in similar circumstances), and therefore produces extensive social services (in non-market or contested market conditions).

• An institutional development that would render a more co-operative functioning of the market economy (including an increasing number of private-public partnerships) attractive.

The New Society scenario basically describes a market economy in which democratic processes dictate regulations and operational constraints in order to meet social objectives.

In this context, for science and technology to develop as required by the private and public innovation processes, the state must consolidate its role as main producer of basic non-appropriable knowledge, and science and technology policy is instrumental to all other collective social policies.

a)   Growth and employment

In the New Society scenario, expected economic growth in the OECD countries could be reduced in comparison with the other scenarios, as the system loses efficiency in favour of greater income equality and more evenly distributed access to the new technologies.

While in principle there is no reason why the innovative capacity of the state in providing social services should be less than the free market alternatives, under this scenario the overall loss of growth potential is linked to the effects of an innovation process more oriented towards user requirements than towards competitiveness. (In fact there are possibilities to be considered in this scenario of organising the state in such a way that it is not isolated from market pressures, for instance by keeping market contestability for its monopolistic powers.)

The public sector assumes leadership in the innovative processes related to a substantial part of the new technologies (particularly IT), as it deals directly with innovation in education, in healthcare, in administrative services, in the administration of justice, in public transportation and communication services, etc. In this scenario, public procurement policies and public R&D policies are the key instruments for the design of a "user-oriented" Information Society.

With a large amount of services remaining outside the market, the "virtuous" growth process expected from a new cluster of technologies is reduced in scope (to the manufacturing and services sectors producing information technology products or marketable information services); this structural consideration confirms that the New Society scenario would also be a low-growth scenario.

In this context it would be difficult to envisage a market solution to the unemployment problem; therefore, this scenario should be associated with regulatory and institutional measures aimed at reducing working hours and redesigning the role of paid work in the social structure,[21] and perhaps even at breaking the linkage between income-generation processes and work (e.g. minimum guaranteed income or a negative income tax).

b) Quality of life and the environment

In the New Society scenario, increasing the quality of life and environmental protection are key objectives for public action. New technologies should be instrumental in fulfilling these objectives; we therefore should expect innovative development of IT, biotechnologies and new materials and energy sources to be closely linked to purposeful public policies.

Of course, these policies include both regulatory measures and public expenditure, and they require finance. The New Society scenario calls for more of an economic role for the state, or at least for a redesign of its activities and sources of finance;[22] ecological taxes could play an important role in this context.

c) Relations with the rest of the world

In the New Society scenario, the OECD countries base their relations with the rest of the world on co-operation rather than competition, thus contributing to more balanced world development. Technology transfer is used as an instrument to improve living conditions in the developing world, and new technologies are also specifically promoted for this purpose; IT is used as a linkage tool. In a way, public action at the world level, guided by OECD initiatives, helps to establish a global solidarity network with financial and technological components.

In general, the New Society scenario envisages a world in which democratic governments assume responsibility for the use of new technologies in the quest for greater global welfare and, by so doing, stimulate the development of these technologies. However, in order to appropriately finance the expenditure required by these new responsibilities, governments need higher direct expenditure. The lack of growth and related public finance is therefore the main bottleneck for the realistic implementation of this scenario.

CONCLUSION: TECHNOLOGY AND THE FUTURE

The cluster of new technologies in the Information Society (computers, telecommunications and microelectronics), biotechnology, new materials and new energy can potentially change all existing production processes and products (both goods and services). The new innovative processes take advantage of several interrelated technological developments, and are themselves deeply interrelated. It is a salient characteristic of the new technological wave that its efficiency increases in complex economic systems.

At the core of this new technological wave are the OECD countries, which are diversified in terms of technological and production capabilities. It is initially in these countries that the greatest gains are expected in terms of both higher quality of life and/or greater production efficiency.

To achieve the positive potential of new technologies, Member countries are faced with the challenge of finding an optimal matching between the technological system and the surrounding social and institutional system.

Scenarios are tools that help to explore alternative futures. Table 2 summarises some aspects of the scenarios considered.

Table 2. **Summary of scenarios**

Issues	Scenarios		
	Market Scenario	Conventional Wisdom	New Society
Growth	Higher	As in the 80's-90's	Lower
Employment	Full employment (dual workforce)	High unemployment	Full employment (work-sharing)
Social cohesion	Growing irregularities	Alternative solutions	High cohesion
Ecological balance	Low priority	Technological solutions	Taxation policies
Relations with rest of the world	De-linking process	Co-operative process	Contractual solidarity
Technology policy	Demand pulled by individual needs	Supply-pushed and demand-pulled	Supply-pushed and demand-pulled by collective needs

The more likely and desirable solutions are to be found between the two extremes of a fully market-driven technological system and a socially controlled technological system. Both these extremes have advantages, but they also have drawbacks that might outweigh those advantages.

Conventional Wisdom therefore tends to consider only small future deviations from the present situation, despite the fact that it already produces some unsatisfactory evaluations (mainly in the areas of employment and income distribution). The fact that some of the new technologies could eliminate the need for instrumental labour within a relatively short period will probably force some fundamental restructuring of social organisations and open more clearly a political debate between alternative views on competition and co-operation as vectors for solving socio-economic conflicts. The debate is already under way in all OECD countries. Some, like the United States, appear to be moving in the direction of a Market scenario; others, like the Netherlands, are introducing institutional changes in the direction of a New Society scenario.

In principle, we could expect higher economic growth from a Market scenario and, since higher economic growth is required to successfully finance a New Society scenario, the Conventional Wisdom scenario (with low economic growth) is still distant from an optimal growth path, considering both alternative and extreme policy points of view. Upgrading the Conventional Wisdom scenario to a higher growth path continues to be the main current economic policy issue. Using technological innovation for this purpose is a challenge for the technology policies of OECD countries. Undoubtedly, technological change stimulates growth by itself; but to change long-term expectations, technology needs further orientation.

An analysis of the alternative Market and New Society scenarios points to some general strategies for upgrading the Conventional Wisdom view in the area of technology policy:

– The Market scenario considers the possibility of more innovative processes adopted by firms in a competitive environment, thus linking deregulation and market-widening to technological change; public technology policy is mainly justified by market failures in the area of basic science and pre-competitive technological research.

– The New Society scenario considers the possibility of stimulating innovative processes mainly to meet collective needs, thus increasing the role of public procurement of science and technology outputs (a role excessively concentrated in defence up to now), and eventually strengthening the production capacity of the public R&D system.

Both these policy considerations are currently contained in Conventional Wisdom approaches. However, policy-makers do not often accept their final implications. Both the Market and New Society scenarios propose more actively demand-pulled technology policies (emerging from either individual or from collective needs). They therefore imply a participatory decision-making process (with firms and with social agents) that often requires deep changes in the traditional process of developing technology policies (excessively dependent on bureaucratic procedures that are heavily influenced by supply-push considerations emerging from the R&D establishment). The use of technology policy as a tool for stimulating economic growth requires that many OECD countries reconsider the premises of today's conventional wisdom as to the way decisions should be made in this field. Increased guidance by anticipation of technological market and collective needs is urgently required if macroeconomic growth is to be seriously enhanced by technology in the future.

NOTES

1. The analysis of long-term fluctuations in economic systems as a result of patterns of technological development has been stimulated in recent years by C. Freeman (1996) and the neo-Schumpeterian and evolutionary schools of economics.

2. In a neoclassical economic context, the rate of change of TFP, also referred to as Solow's residual, is defined as:

    $$\hat{r} = \hat{q} - a\hat{l} - (1-a)\hat{k}$$

    where the superscript hat (^) indicates the relative rate of change, (r) is TFP, (q) is net output in value-added terms, (l) is labour input, (k) capital input and (a) the share of wages in total output.

    In the input-output framework, the notion of gross products allows for the introduction of intermediate inputs together with the primary inputs (Wolff, 1997).

3. Researchers from the OECD have conducted several studies on TFP growth. Recent results have been reported in Sakurai et al., 1997. A view of the OECD secretariat research results in the broader area of technology diffusion, productivity, employment and skills and international competitiveness is provided in OECD, 1996.

4. Following pioneering work by E. Mansfield and Z. Griliches, the relation between R&D (generally separating basic from applied R&D) and TFP growth has been thoroughly explored, and estimates are available for rates of return on R&D investments computed as a_1 in the equation

    TFPGRT = a_0 + a_1 RDGDP + e

    where TFPGRT is the rate of growth of TFP, and RDGDP is the ratio of R&D expenditure to GDP. These rates of return are usually estimated in the range of 10 to 30 per cent.

    Concerning the process of human capital accumulation, authors generally prefer to follow Denison, Griliches, Kendrick and Jorgenson, and directly introduce the changes in the quality of labour in the labour component of the production function, or include education as one of the factors in a growth accounting context.

5. Based on the initial concept of core competence developed by Hamel and Prahalad (1990), the identification of the three components of technological, human and organisational competences is developed in Bueno, Morcillo and Rodriguez, 1997.

6. Carter (1994) introduces the concept that pursuing innovation is itself an economic activity with costs and investment requirements: "firms acquire intangible capital by hiring appropriate individuals and providing them with whatever materials and equipment they need to acquire information, organise networks, etc. The cumulated expenses of these wages, materials and equipment is intangible investment... Change-oriented investment extends well beyond formal R&D to include organisational and reputational investment, establishing and fine-tuning supplier and sales networks, inter-firm co-operation and support for complementary products appropriate to the current production set."

7. The pioneering work of D. Aschauer (1989, pp. 177-200) started an empirical controversy on the contribution of public capital stock to TFP growth; in general, the results both in the United States and in Europe point to the existence of a positive causal linkage.

8. The question of measuring institutional aspects of the process of technological change has received little attention; we can still quote the results of Nadiri's (1970) survey – "We need to know the contribution of government services like laws, regulations, etc. to the growth of factor productivity" – as a sensible recommendation.

9. A special issue of *Economic Systems Research* on intersectoral R&D spillovers (1997) collects several recent studies on technological spillovers; empirical results confirm the very important role played by indirect R&D (that performed by suppliers of intermediate inputs or capital equipment) in the overall innovative performance of any single industry. The paper by E.N. Wolff in this same issue of ESR, "Spillovers, Linkages and Technical Change", also finds strong evidence, using US data, that "industry TFP growth is significantly related to the TFP performance of supplying sectors, with an elasticity of almost 60 per cent". Wolff concludes: "The new results presented here strongly suggest that, within manufacturing at least, a decline in TFP growth in an industry can pull down the technological growth of associated industries." Rather similar results for several OECD countries are provided by Papaconstantinou, Sakurai and Wyckoff (1996). These authors indicate that "the part of total technology embodied in output which is acquired externally has increased over time...The distinction between high, medium and low technology industries blurs when accounting for the purchase of technologically sophisticated inputs...The analysis revealed that while innovations are developed mainly in a cluster of high technology manufacturing industries, the main acquirers of technologically sophisticated machinery and equipment are a different cluster of industries in the services sector."

10. The analysis of the distributional effects of TFP gains, in particular as a function of market structure, is developed by Carter (1990) and by Fontela (1994a).

11. This idea is also developed in Appelbaum and Schettkat (1994), and by the same authors in Paper FS I 93-313, Wissenschaftszentrum Berlin für Sozialforschung, comparing data for Germany, Japan, Sweden and the United States.

12. Of particular importance for the analysis of the matching process between technological and social change is the work of Perez (1983).

13. Baumol (1967, pp. 415-426) concluded his analysis of a dichotomous economy with progressive and relatively constant productivity sectors as follows: "Our model tells us that manufactures are likely to continue to decline in relative cost and, unless the income elasticity of demand for manufactured goods is very large, they may absorb an even smaller proportion of the labour force, which, if it transpires, may make it more difficult for our economy to maintain its overall rate of output growth." This long-term asymptotic evolution towards lower economic growth is known as "Baumol's Disease".

14. Using US data for the period 1947-76, Baumol, Batey Blackman and Wolff (1985, pp. 806-817) showed that "The output shares of the progressive and stagnant sectors have in fact remained fairly constant in the post-war period, so that with rising relative prices, the share of total expenditures of the (stagnant) services and their share of the labour force have risen dramatically (their prices rose at about the same rate as their productivity lagged behind the progressive sectors) just as the model suggests." The authors also found evidence of "asymptotically stagnant activities" in some high-tech sectors (such as TV broadcasting and electronic computation) that "contain both a technologically sophisticated component and a relatively irreducible labour-intensive component", thus suggesting that "the progressivity of such activities may well prove transitory and somewhat illusory".

15. Twenty years ago, INTERFUTURES, an OECD study about long-term trends in Member countries and their relations with the rest of the world, pioneered the area of scenario-building (OECD, 1979). The OECD International Futures Programme continuously updates a documentation system providing key findings of literature selected from the worldwide output of future analysis (*Future Trends*, OECD, Paris). In *Societal Cohesion and the Globalising Economy* (OECD, 1997), scenarios are used to explore further alternatives in the relation between social cohesion and the development model. In that book's opening chapter, Michalski, Miller and Stevens (1997) – after projecting incremental changes to the welfare state – explore two alternative scenarios: an Individualistic scenario, which radically reduces the role of governments in all domains, and a Solidaristic scenario, which depends heavily on strong collective institutions and shared values. In many respects, this analysis is consistent with the Conventional Wisdom ("business as usual" projection), Market and New Society scenarios considered in this paper.

16. CEPII (1996) has published a summary of a research project performed for the EC (DG XVII) dealing with the macroeconomic framework for long-term energy projections.

17. A more comprehensive description of the technological aspects of a scenario based on current expert opinion is to be found in Northcott's (1991) *Britain in 2010* – especially in Part I, dealing with "The World in 2010".

18. Fontela (1994b) defines the employment issue as follows: "most manufacturing and many services (notably network services) have reached or are reaching peak employment and are likely to require less labour in the future".

19. A Market scenario is described by Northcott (1991, p. 320) as follows: "This Scenario is designed to illustrate the effects of 'right' policies intended to give freer play to market forces, with more deregulation and privatisation, lower taxes and substantial further cuts in public expenditure." Along similar lines, Shell International Petroleum, in its

Global Scenarios 1992-2020 (1993), studies a scenario in which the success of liberalisation policies generates pressures towards more liberalisation, permanently opening new opportunities for investment and trade. In Michalski, Miller and Stevens (1997), the Individualistic Scenario states that "radically reducing the role of governments in all domains — social programmes, economic regulation, public enterprises — offers a fairly direct path to greater flexibility in the allocation of resources by individuals and firms".

20. It could be said that a New Society scenario supported by technological developments has indeed been explored over a number of years (1979-1994) within the framework of FAST — Forecasting and Assessment in the field of Science and Technology, DG XII, Commission of the European Union. Practically all relevant aspects of social change in relation to new technologies have been analysed (mostly by European researchers) within this programme.

21. Whereas 150 years ago, with a life expectancy at birth of 57 years, an industrial worker used to spend 66 per cent of his/her available time (after deduction of childhood and physical rest during lifetime) at the factory, today this percentage varies between 15 and 20 per cent in the OECD countries and is constantly declining due to the reduction in the average number of years worked in a lifetime and to the increase in life expectancy. A greater integration of work, education and leisure is now certainly possible but requires new institutional developments (e.g. in continuing education).

22. The New Society scenario may include major changes in the tax structure (e.g. giving a key role to taxes on negative environmental externalities, or to taxes on information flows) and, more generally, in the income-generating processes of public institutions (e.g. economically exploiting commons such as water). Current methods of financing the state were developed in the framework of the industrial society, and are not necessarily well adapted to the coming Information Society.

BIBLIOGRAPHY

APPELBAUM, E. and R. SCHETTKAT (1994), "The End of Full Employment? On Economic Development in Industrialised Countries", *Intereconomics,* May/June, pp. 122-130.

ASCHAUER, D. (1989), "Is Public Expenditure Productive?", *Journal of Monetary Economics*, 23, March.

BAUMOL, W.J. (1967), "Macroeconomics of Unbalanced Growth: The Anatomy of Urban Crisis", *American Economic Review*, 57, June.

BAUMOL, W.J., S.A. BATEY BLACKMAN and E.N. WOLFF (1985), "Unbalanced Growth Revisited: Asymptotic Stagnancy and New Evidence", *American Economic Review*, Vol. 75, No. 4, September.

BUENO, E., P. MORCILLO and J.M. RODRIGUEZ (1997), "Management of Technology: Proposal for a Diagnosis Model", *The Journal of High Technology Management Research*, Arizona State University, Vol. 8, No. 1.

CARTER, Anne P. (1990), "Upstream and Downstream Benefits of Innovation", *Economic Systems Research*, Vol. 2, No. 3, pp. 241-257.

CARTER, Anne P. (1994), "Change as Economic Activity", Brandeis University Department of Economics.

CEPII – Centre d'Études Prospectives et d'Information Internationales (1996), *La Lettre du CEPII*, 148, Paris, July.

Economic Systems Research (1997), Special Issue on Intersectoral R&D Spillovers, co-ordinated by P. Mohnen, Vol. 9., No. 1, March. Includes paper by E.N. Wolff, "Spillovers, Linkages and Technical Change".

FONTELA, E. (1994*a*), "Inter-industry Distribution of Productivity Gains", *Economic Systems Research*, Vol. 6, No. 3, pp. 227-236.

FONTELA, E. (1994*b*), "The Long-term Outlook for Growth and Employment", *OECD Societies in Transition: The Future of Work and Leisure,* OECD, Paris.

FREEMAN, Christopher, ed. (1996), *Long Wave Theory*, The International Library of Critical Writings in Economics, 69, Edward Elgar Publishing, Cheltenham (UK), Lynne (US).

HAMEL, G. and C.K. PRAHALAD (1990), "The Core Competence of the Corporation", *Harvard Business Review*, Vol. 68, No. 3.

MICHALSKI, W., R. MILLER and B. STEVENS (1997), "Economic Flexibility and Societal Cohesion in the Twenty-first Century: An Overview of the Issues and Key Points of the Discussion", *Societal Cohesion and the Globalising Economy*, OECD, Paris.

NADIRI, M.I. (1970), "Some Approaches to the Theory and Measurement of Total Factor Productivity: A Survey", *Journal of Economic Literature*, VIII, 4, pp. 1137-77.

NORTHCOTT, J. (1991), *Britain in 2010*, The Policy Studies Institute, London. Part 1: "The World in 2010".

OECD (1979), *Facing the Future: Mastering the Probable and Managing the Unpredictable* (the INTERFUTURES Project), OCED, Paris.

OECD (1996), *Technology and Industrial Performance*, Paris.

OECD (1997), *Societal Cohesion and the Globalising Economy*, Paris.

PAPACONSTANTINOU, G., N. SAKURAI and A. WYCKOFF (1996), "Embodied Technology Diffusion: An Empirical Analysis for 10 OECD Countries", *Technology and Industrial Performance,* OECD, Paris.

PEREZ, C. (1983), "Structural Change and Assimilation of New Technologies in the Economic and Social Systems", *Futures*, Vol. 15, No. 5, pp. 357-376.

SAKURAI, N., G. PAPACONSTANTINOW and E. IOANNIDIS (1997), "Impact of R&D and Technology Diffusion on Productivity Growth: Empirical Evidence for 10 OECD Countries", *Economic Systems Research*, Vol. 9, No. 1, pp. 81-109.

SHELL INTERNATIONAL PETROLEUM (1993), *Global Scenarios 1992-2020*, London.

WOLFF, Edward N., ed. (1997), "The Economics of Productivity (I and II)", The International Library of Critical Writings in Economics, 77, Edward Elgar Publishing, Cheltenham (UK), Lynne (US). See also *Economic Systems Research*, 1997.

7

GLOBAL POSSIBILITIES: TECHNOLOGY AND PLANET-WIDE CHALLENGES

by

Luc Soete

Maastricht Economic Research Institute on Innovation and Technology (MERIT),
University of Limburg, The Netherlands

INTRODUCTION

There is little doubt that, viewed in retrospect, the last ten years have been a period of historic structural transformation at the world level: the collapse of the former communist countries and their rapid opening up to market-led economic incentives; the shift in world market growth from the old North Atlantic OECD area to the Pacific basin area; the liberalisation of financial capital markets bringing about *de facto* the international mobility of capital; and the dramatic reduction in the costs of information and communication processing, opening up an increasing number of sectors to international trade and giving at least the impression of a dramatic reduction in physical distances – the world as a village.

This fast-paced global restructuring process raises some fundamental policy challenges at national – and European – policy levels. It has made decision-makers much more aware of the increased international implications of their policy actions. Policies that might appear "sustainable" within a national (or even European) context may now seem less so in a global context. While the full impact of opening up to international restructuring (manufactured goods, some services) may only be felt in the next century, it is already clear that the scope for national policy action has been dramatically reduced in many different fields. This holds not only for traditional macroeconomic policy, but also for social, tax, social security and other policies traditionally pursued at the national level.

Parenthetically, it is interesting to observe that these globalisation trends also raise some fundamental challenges with regard to Europe's own integration process. The aims of that process increasingly appear to be overtaken, in both concept and speed of implementation, by those of the broader worldwide integration process. [The WTO Singapore agreement on the liberalisation of information technology trade comes to mind.] It could well be asked whether the process of European economic integration – where the central aim is the reaping of the scale advantages of a 350-million-consumer market – is not, at least in the area of manufactured goods, entering into a phase of decreasing marginal return, and in need of new policy reflection and possible policy action in the next century (Soete, 1997).

In a first, short section of this paper some of the main features of globalisation linked to new information and communication technologies (ICTs) are discussed. Without wishing to minimise the importance of some of the other aspects of worldwide structural change, these technologies appear to have been a central "engine" in the acceleration of the globalisation process. In many ways, ICTs represent historically the first "global" technological transformation to confront our societies (OECD, 1996).

In the three sections that follow, the analysis shifts to the various ways in which global conditions appear to interact with the emergence and use of new technologies. There is little doubt that most of the solutions to our current and future global economic, social and environmental problems will have to be found in the more efficient use of new technologies: in food production and distribution; in environmentally friendly (recycling, clean and zero emission) techniques; in renewable energy; in more efficient and less polluting transport systems of goods and persons; in health and disease prevention; etc. The large social returns to public and private investment in such areas transcend national borders. It is particularly from this perspective that the traditional national focus of science and technology inherited from a postwar and/or cold war mentality appears out of place and based on short-term national interests.

Section 2 explores the interactions between countries' growth dynamics and firms' innovative and technological capabilities as they have evolved in an increasingly global environment. What emerges from the analysis is the complexity of the science and technology institutional framework, what has been described as the national system of innovation (Freeman, 1987, Lundvall, 1992, Nelson, 1992). The effectiveness of such national institutional frameworks is clearly being challenged by the increasingly global behaviour of private firms but also by the growing role and importance of regional conditions, including regional policy-making, for creating and maintaining advantage based on location.

What, then, continues to justify national policy-making in this area? Section 3 briefly outlines some of the main policy arguments with respect to technology support policies and "international competitiveness". The voluminous literature, not reviewed here,[1] points to the variety of conditions with respect to both the nature of the new technology (radical, incremental) and the different sectors (science-based, process-oriented, etc.) likely to come into play and their normative, national policy implications. This variety of conditions is reflected in an impressive variety of national institutional set-ups governing the creation and diffusion of innovation and technological capabilities. However, it also highlights the difficulties in identifying "best practice" policy.[2] Hence, despite the obvious advantages to international co-operation of establishing some "global level playing field" in this area, the issue of policy competition versus harmonization remains open to debate.[3]

Section 4 shifts the analysis to a global problem area which at least on paper appears less controversial: the development and worldwide diffusion of environmentally sustainable technologies. This is the prime example of an area where policy-makers will increasingly be confronted with the need for joint policy action in the next century. They will clearly require an international version of the traditional national toolbox of policy instruments (direct regulation, economic instruments and public procurement).

As the case of environmental technologies well illustrates, many of the challenges of globalisation raise questions about global democratic control, even global revenue-raising capacity, both of which are mentioned in the Conclusion. Transforming the current deregulation trend – inspired by the liberalisation and opening up of many new sectors to international competition – into a process of more positive integration, including fund-raising, represents one of the most fundamental challenges for the next century. Such positive integration, in order to be successful, will have to deal not only with the many countries' and regions' conflicting interests in a wide variety of areas – it will also have to recognise fully the interests of future generations.

1. GLOBALISATION AND INFORMATION AND COMMUNICATION TECHNOLOGIES

As in many other areas of structural change, there is an ongoing debate about the factual evidence surrounding globalisation.[4] Most of the evidence readily available focuses on trade and foreign direct investment flows (OECD, 1993). This evidence tends to suggest that there has been little increase in globalisation. Imports into the EU from some of the new entrants [the newly industrialising countries (NICs), some of the other Asian economies, East European economies in transition] have increased rapidly over the last twenty years, but not to such an extent as to explain in any way a structural break from the past. Similarly, foreign direct investment flows still only represent a small fraction of total investment in OECD countries. Clearly, such measures of international flows reflect only one limited feature of "globalisation". Growth in the globalisation of financial flows over the last two decades, for example, has been dramatic. Cross-border transactions in bonds and equities have increased in OECD countries over the last fifteen years from 10 per cent of GDP in 1980 to between 150 and 250 per cent of

GDP in 1995. At the same time, the worldwide volume of foreign exchange trading has increased to a turnover of more than $1.2 trillion a day (according to the BIS 1996 Annual Report). Growth in the exchange of information that has become instantaneously and globally available can, on the other hand, only be guessed. There is little doubt that the world has indeed entered into something of a new era in which global access has become the major characteristic of both production and consumption.

At the centre of this process is of course the cluster of new information and communication technologies and their ability to reduce communication and information handling and processing costs dramatically. While it might be something of a misnomer to talk about "global" access in a world in which half the population has no direct access to public telephony, there is nonetheless a trend towards worldwide access that is intrinsically linked with the ability of ICTs to transmit information and knowledge over both distance and time. In some areas (such as finance), where this process has been accompanied by institutional liberalisation and deregulation, the globalisation process has been far more rapid and is nearly complete: financial capital has in essence become an internationally mobile production factor. In traditional manufacturing production, the decline in communication and information costs has further increased the transparency of markets worldwide, reinforcing the scope for international location. In areas such as services, new ICTs are – often for the first time – allowing cheap global access to low-cost labour locations, thus facilitating the relocation of various "routine" service functions and activities. Firms and organisations have come to discover the benefits of international differences in labour costs in areas hitherto limited in their international tradability (Freeman and Soete, 1994).

In other words, ICTs contribute to global economic transparency and – in so far as they bring to the forefront the cost advantages of alternative locations – to international capital mobility and "outsourcing" of particular activities. Furthermore, ICTs have positively affected international access to information and "codified" knowledge (David and Foray, 1995). That knowledge, which includes the economic knowledge of markets, becomes to some extent available on a worldwide basis. While the local capacities to use or transform codified knowledge will vary widely, the potential for access is there. ICTs thus represent the potential for catching up, based upon the economic transparency of advantages, while stressing the crucial "tacit" and other competency elements required to access internationally codified knowledge (Foray and Lundvall, 1996; OECD, 1996). It is important in this context to emphasize at the outset the undisputed benefits of a more transparent, borderless global economy – the international economist's dream. To some extent, the new ICTs are making that dream possible by producing economic incentives that allow countries to converge more rapidly, and thus help bring about a more equal level of development around the globe.

2. "GLOBAL" FIRMS, TECHNOLOGICAL CAPABILITIES AND COUNTRIES' GROWTH DYNAMICS

The structural change pressures described above have led to a shift in the *form* of globalisation. Apart from that induced by rapid international financial liberalisation, globalisation indeed no longer seems simply a question of "globalising" sales with accompanying services such as marketing, distribution and after-sales service, but involves to a greater extent production, including production of component suppliers; investment, including intangible investment; merger acquisitions, partnerships and so-called "strategic" alliances; etc.

As discussed in many recent contributions in the international business literature (among others Narula, 1996 and Pavitt and Patel, 1998), the aims of firms are increasingly directed towards global presence strategies that strike a balance between, on the one hand, reaping some of the scale advantages of global markets increasingly associated with intangibles (research, communication, marketing, logistics, management), and on the other exploiting the (often geographically determined) diversity of consumers and production factors. The large multinational firm's organisational as well as production technology will give it the necessary flexibility to confront this diversity. The decentralisation of its production units and even new product development, together with a diversification of subcontractors, will enable it to take full advantage of that same diversity. This explains the apparent contradictory "glocalisation" trend: physical presence under what appears sometimes rather "autarkic" production conditions in the various large trade blocs (EU, NAFTA, ASEAN, China) with often highly differentiated "local" products yet increasing global exchange of some of the core technological competences of the firm through, *e.g.*, the establishment of alliances or networking with other firms.

The actual location of the "multi-domestic" firm's plant will depend heavily on local conditions. The choice will often depend on the availability of local skills, infrastructure, and access to knowledge; at the same time, the firm itself will of course contribute to the long-term growth and availability of human resources, access to knowledge, local suppliers' know-how and networks. These often scarce and sometimes geographically "fixed" factors contribute to the creation of increasing returns to growth features of long-term development (Arthur, 1995).

Such apparently opposing trends raise a number of important policy issues, not least with respect to the level at which policy should be implemented so as to be most effective. It is obvious that global or multi-domestic firms increasingly question the meaning of *national* policies. In many cases such firms might display just as much "good citizenship" as national firms; in other cases they might not. It is difficult if not impossible for governments to draw lines here: the current OECD guidelines with respect to foreign direct investment provide little more than a voluntary "standard" of good international behaviour.

Following the OECD TEP programme of the late 1980s (OECD, 1991, 1992), proposals were made to establish, for national policy purposes, a way of measuring the "degree of globalisation" of firms, *e.g.* in terms of the composition of boards, the international breakdown of key management posts and of research laboratories, and – more generally – physical and intangible investment. Given the ongoing debate in the literature on the extent and nature of "globalisation", such a measure could be useful in assessing mergers and acquisitions, particularly in areas which had received national industrial and technology support: if firm A with a foreign headquarters was judged to have a low degree of globalisation, then a national firm that was integrated into A could be described as coming under foreign control. By contrast, a national firm with a low degree of globalisation that became part of a more global company might be provided with new, global market opportunities.

But it will also be obvious from the description above that any such measures are likely to become quickly eroded by the many practical ways in which explicit expressions of globalisation can be faked or hidden. Obviously a more international policy response is necessary[5] – and that need for international rules of the game, in particular with respect to competition policy, arises precisely from national differences and the absence of an international regime for overseeing transnational investment, acquisitions and mergers. At the risk of increasingly becoming a source of conflict in the few areas of international harmonization and institutional authority that do exist (such as trade policy and the WTO), such international policy should aim at counteracting the emergence of worldwide cartels between global firms; reduce the divergence between national competition policies; and monitor more closely the degree and extent of firms' globalisation.

At the same time, and perhaps paradoxically, the multi-domestic firm also questions the relevance of national-policy making from a regional, local perspective. As indicated above, multi-domestic firms will both take advantage of and contribute to the emergence of the infrastructural advantage of location. Particularly important in this context is infrastructure linked to the innovation system. This is the infrastructure that provides the major incentives for private investment in intangible (including human) resources and for linking up with public research institutes – possibly for setting up specialised centres of excellence, training partnerships, technical information agencies, etc. In other words, it is this infrastructure that can lead to a local *interactive* learning cluster, possibly even the establishment of a global "competence centre" in a particular product or market niche.

The effective exploitation of as well as contribution to such locally created advantages by multi-domestic firms again raises a number of important policy issues. At the site level this might often translate into rivalries concerning the services offered to firms, and there will in effect be no limit to the bidding. As a result, there is, as is evident from the European experience, a multiplicity of new growth sites, science parks and technopoli being set up; none developing the size necessary to reach some of the essential externalities and increasing return growth features, and all increasing the cost of communicating and interacting.

The desire of local authorities to attract such high-tech learning centres illustrates to some extent the further erosion – and relevance – of national policy-making in this area. Nowhere is this becoming more obvious than in cross-border peripheral regions, where the national central interests are unlikely to coincide with local interest. In South Limburg in the Netherlands, for example, national policy- and priority-setting, *e.g.* with respect to infrastructure or foreign investment attraction, is increasingly perceived as a form of *"randstaddemocratie"* – a term used by the Chairman of the local Chamber of Commerce. While the intensification of global competition has made the role of regional conditions, including regional policy, more important, the individual citizen is increasingly identifying such local conditions – the quality of the environment, children's education, availability of social and cultural services – as the essential features of his or her welfare and quality of life. Hence, there is growing political pressure for decentralisation or devolution of policy responsibilities, including necessary financial means, away from the national centre towards local communities (regions, cities, etc.). With the erosion in national government responsibilities, citizens themselves increasingly appear to be requesting that a larger part of their national tax payments contribute directly to the improvement of their local living conditions. The effectiveness of such policies could then also be assessed in a much more direct and immediate way.

3. NATIONAL TECHNOLOGY SUPPORT POLICIES AND INTERNATIONAL COMPETITIVENESS

From a national policy perspective, economic and social progress can be said to depend on widespread capacity to compete in increasingly global markets, and on the dynamic turnover of winners and losers as efficiency in exploiting new economic opportunities shifts between enterprises and nations. This has been to some extent the bread and butter of national economic policy. The competitiveness question is whether technology is today such an important element in the process of structural change and globalisation that differences in the capacity to bring technology into the market are a matter of priority concern for enterprises and governments. Also, is it simply a matter of enterprise strategies and capabilities, or do public authorities need to intervene to ensure that *their* enterprises can compete in the international market?

The old debate about different North American, European and Asian capabilities can be seen in this light. It is not so much an issue of access to technology but one of the capacity to innovate and to diffuse technology. These capacities, then, depend on a wide range of conditions and institutions, some of which might be strongly influenced by government policy – but the essential feature of success is likely to be entrepreneurship, and involve technology, management and financial innovation.

Given the great variety of institutional set-ups, can one identify some regularities across industries and countries? In order to provide some tentative answers, it is essential – as has been pointed out by many economists in the (neo-)Schumpeterian tradition (from Dosi, 1984 to Howitt, 1996) – to distinguish between "normal" technical progress, which proceeds along the trajectories defined by an established paradigm, and those "extraordinary" technological advances that relate to the emergence of radically new paradigms.

As regards the latter, it is generally acknowledged that market processes are usually weak in directing the emergence and selection of these radical technological discontinuities. When the process of innovation is highly exploratory, its direct responsiveness to economic signals is rather loose and the linkages with strictly scientific knowledge quite strong. In such cases non-market organisations appear to have played an important role, often providing the necessary conditions for new scientific developments and performing as *ex ante* selectors of the explored technological paradigm among all the other potential ones. Here, the case of the semiconductor and computer technologies comes to mind, and the influence of both military agencies and big electrical corporations in the early days of these radically new technologies. Somewhat similar cases can be found in the early developments of synthetic chemistry,[6] or more recently the development of bioengineering, new materials or even the Internet.

The institutional and scientific contexts and existing public policy are fundamental in the search and selection of new technological paradigms; they affect *a*) the bridging mechanisms between pure science and technological developments, *b*) the search criteria and capabilities of economic agents, and *c*) the constraints, incentives and uncertainty facing would-be innovators.

Similarly, at the international level, when new technologies emerge, the relative success of the various countries or regions will depend on the successful matching between each country's scientific context and technological capabilities; the nature of their "bridging institutions"; economic conditions (relative prices, the nature and size of the markets, availability/scarcity of raw materials, etc.); and the nature of the dominant rules of behaviour, strategies and forms of organisation of the economic actors. All these variables are also – but to different degrees – affected by public policies, either directly (*e.g.* procurement policies or R&D subsidies which obviously influence the economic signals facing individual firms) or indirectly (*e.g.* through the educational system's influence on scientific and technological capabilities, the effect of taxation policies on the emergence of new firms, etc.).

As concerns "normal" technical progress, the variety in the organisational patterns of innovative activities is of course much greater, and makes it difficult to draw general trends. Two, however, have been highlighted in the literature.

First, the balance between what is co-ordinated and organised through the visible hand of corporate structures and what is left to the invisible hand of the markets depends on both the technology and the country (Pavitt, 1984, Tidd *et al.*, 1997). In science-based industries, for instance, whenever technological paradigms become established, the process of Schumpeterian competition tends to produce rather big oligopolies which also internalise considerable innovative capabilities (*e.g.* computers, semiconductors, synthetic chemicals, software, content, etc.). In production-intensive industries, the "visible hand" of big corporations, in somewhat similar fashion, puts the organisation of technological advances at the core of their strategic behaviour (*e.g.* automobiles, most other consumer durables, etc.). In the case of specialised suppliers, technological advances are generally organised through matching their own specific technological skills and intense (often arm's-length and untraded) relationships with users or component producers. Finally, only in supplier-dominated sectors do the mechanisms of organisation and co-ordination of technological progress appear to retain some significant similarities with the classical view of the "invisible hand": technological advances are generally available on the market in the form of new capital goods, there are many firms with weak strategic interactions, etc.

Second, there are significant intersectoral differences in the balance between public institutions and private organisations in the process of innovation (Mansfield, 1995). Some sectors rely on an endogenous process of technological advance, while others depend heavily on public sources of innovation. Dosi, Pavitt and Soete (1990) suggested the following empirical generalisation: the higher the role of the visible hand of oligopolistic organisations, the lower the requirement for strictly public institutions in the processes of economic co-ordination and technological advance. And the reverse also holds: the nearer one activity is to "pure competition", the higher its need for strictly institutional forms of organisation of its externalities and technological advances. Agriculture is a well-known case in point: historically, a significant part of its technological advance, at least in the United States, has been provided by government-sponsored research. By contrast, many oligopoly-dominated manufacturing sectors have produced a good part of their "normal" technological advance endogenously, and have appeared to co-ordinate their price/quantity adjustments rather well.

The foregoing discussion suggests that in the postwar economic development of OECD countries, non-market agencies have been a major actor in the emergence of new technological paradigms, but at the same time the conditions of technological opportunity and appropriability have guaranteed rather sustained rates of "normal" technical progress, endogenously generated through oligopolistic manufacturing corporations. It is important to note, however, that every government has intervened – in forms and degrees that depended on the sectors and countries – so as to strengthen the incentives to innovate.

Confronted with this variety of factors and actors, can one make any normative statement linking institutional forms, degrees of public involvement and economic performance that might be of relevance to a discussion of future growth and development paths? In a changing complex world such as the one under analysis here, reaching definite conclusions on national "optimal" set-ups is practically impossible. At best, one can define some trade-offs involved in each organisational configuration. Within the context of technology policy, three such trade-offs appear essential. First, at the very core of the innovative process undertaken by profit-motivated agents, there is necessarily some sort of "market failure" in a static sense. Varying degrees of appropriability are the necessary incentive to innovate, but at the same time they imply "excess profits" and "sub-optimal" allocation of resources. Best-practice techniques and better products diffuse throughout the (national and international) economy after an interval, and the gap between the technological frontier and the infra-marginal techniques also measures to some extent the static inefficiency of any pattern of allocation of resources.[7]

Asymmetries in capabilities are a direct consequence of the partly appropriable nature of technological advances. They also correspond to an asymmetric pattern of economic signals, so that high technological opportunity, associated with a high degree of appropriability of technological innovation, may well perform as a powerful incentive to innovate for a company at or near the technological frontier. At the same time, such technological opportunities will be a powerful negative signal (i.e. an entry barrier) for a company with relatively lower technological capability. The current development of the software industry, with its geographical concentration in the United States (Steinmueller, 1996) following the increasingly successful enforcement of intellectual property worldwide, is an excellent illustration.

A second normative issue concerns the ways in which each society builds its technological capabilities and translates these into innovative entrepreneurial behaviour. Again, one observes a wide international variance in both the "supply of entrepreneurship" and the ways it is institutionally formed. The difference between the organised entrepreneurship of Japanese firms and the self-made-man archetype in the United States is a typical example; so is that between the formalized "production" of technological/managerial capabilities in France (the Ecole Polytechnique, etc.) and the anarchic Italian pattern. Many historians have provided vivid descriptions of the growth of American technocracy, that highlight the enormous changes which the contemporary economies have undergone since the times of the "classical" Protestant capitalist studied by Weber in *The Protestant Ethic and the Spirit of Capitalism*. Yet more international studies on the training mechanisms of managers/technocrats/entrepreneurs would be needed in order to understand the social supply in various countries of this crucial factor in innovative activities. The EU policy call for more entrepreneurship (one of the recommendations of the Jobs Summit in Luxembourg – see European Union, 1997) should be understood in this context.

A third normative issue concerns the possible trade-off between allocative efficiency and flexibility, or, more generally speaking, between "fitness" for a particular state-of-the-world and the capability of coping with other (unpredictable) environments. One can detect here an analogy with biological evolution. Extreme optimisation within a given environment might well imply a "dinosaur syndrome" and inflexibility to change. Conversely, high adaptability is likely to involve waste, "slack", and sub-optimal use of resources.

There is little doubt that the current diffusion of new information and communication technologies has substantially shifted the trade-offs between flexibility and economies of scale, increasing flexibility, lowering the minimum throughputs which allow for automated processes, and shortening product life cycles. There is today a far greater need for variety in capabilities, behavioural rules and allocative processes that might allow for greater adaptability to uncertainty and change. One of the greatest strengths of capitalism has been its capability of continuously producing redundant resources, of exploring an "excessive" number of technological trajectories, of producing a wasteful number of technological/organisational "genotypes". In a sense – and contrary to the old general equilibrium notion – if there is some advantage of contemporary market economies over centrally planned ones, it is probably the fact that the former precisely do not achieve an equilibrium of the Arrow-Debreu kind but are highly imperfect and always characterised by allocative inefficiencies and technological slacks.

The policy questions are consequently – and not surprisingly – rather complex. How can a sufficient "variety" be continuously generated? On the other hand, how can the potential of new technologies be better realised? To what extent is the realisation of such potential primarily dependent on individual entrepreneurship and risk-taking? Is the current move towards a more stringent enforceable appropriation regime worldwide (in patent law, copyrights, authors' rights) slowing down international technology diffusion and raising technology-related monopoly rents? These issues become even more entangled in open economies, let alone in the increasingly global "planet" environment of the 21st century.

The global trends described above call for much more active and explicit international co-ordination; setting of priorities at the world level in the area of science and technology; and even guarantees of some degree of variety in a world of globalised communication and information. At a general level, there is little doubt that once the complexity of science and technology is taken into account in all its dimensions, the advantages of *international* interaction, networking and co-ordination (as is *de facto* taking place in the private sector with respect to privately funded research) of government-sponsored basic and long-term research become self-evident. With the research costs in many areas rising, it is obvious that international co-ordination and collaboration represent a more efficient way of reaping the potential benefits of *both* national and world research efforts.

Not surprisingly, these global advantages have been most evident in the case of the so-called "big science" research efforts, where no single country or even triad bloc can any longer cover the full variety and diversity of scientific disciplines, approaches and methodologies, let alone the rapidly increasing equipment and material costs of such research. An interesting question is whether the richest, most developed countries do not also have a responsibility for international burden-sharing of such "big science" research efforts. There are major differences between, *e.g.*, the OECD countries in the amount of public resources devoted to basic research. Such differences are not always closely related to the income levels of such countries, nor to their growth rate. Nevertheless, without going into the international "free rider" debate about science and knowledge flows, the question of more explicit "global" responsibility must be asked. That responsibility comes even more to the forefront once the "global" demand side and the truly global environmental problems confronting the world are introduced into the analysis – and in the larger sense that category of problem could include famine, diseases, desertification, energy, etc. In each of these areas it could be said that the social rate of return to the world as a whole is higher than the individual country's. Compared to the potential waste of resources at the world level because of duplication of effort, co-ordination of research activities beyond national prestige must here be an absolute priority.

4. WORLDWIDE TECHNOLOGY CO-OPERATION AND SUSTAINABLE DEVELOPMENT

From many perspectives, global involvement and active use of science and technology policies to achieve environmental goals should constitute the new focus and priority for technology policy. At first sight, this would seem to require a return to the emphasis of the 1950s and 1960s on public goals that were met through mission-oriented projects, now with a more explicit global focus. However, there is a fundamental difference between these older projects – *e.g.* nuclear, defence and aerospace programmes – and new projects to support environmentally sustainable development. The former aimed at the development of radically new technologies through government procurement that was largely isolated from the rest of the economy, though they frequently affected the structure of some industries and could lead to new spin-off technologies that had widespread effects on other sectors. In contrast with that earlier notion, the new "mission-oriented" environmental projects will need to combine procurement with many other policies in order to have pervasive effects on the entire structure of production and consumption within the economy.

Hence, the pervasive character of new projects to meet environmental goals calls for a more systemic approach to policy. Table 1 (from Freeman and Soete, 1997) summarises the key characteristics and differences between the old and new models of mission-oriented projects.

Table 1. **Characteristics of old and new "mission-oriented" projects**

Old: defence, nuclear and aerospace	New: environmental technologies
The mission is defined in terms of the number and type of technical achievements with little regard to their economic feasibility.	The mission is defined in terms of economically feasible technical solutions to particular environmental problems.
• The goals and the direction of technological development are defined in advance by a small group of experts.	• The direction of technical change is influenced by a wide range of actors including government, private firms and consumer groups.
• Centralised control within a government administration.	• Decentralised control with a large number of agents involved.
• Diffusion of the results outside the core of participants is of minor importance or actively discouraged.	• Diffusion of the results is a central goal and is actively encouraged.
• Limited to a small group of firms that can participate owing to the emphasis on a small number of radical technologies.	• An emphasis on the development of both radical and incremental innovations in order to permit a large number of firms to participate.
• Self-contained projects with little need for complementary policies and scant attention paid to coherence.	• Complementary policies vital for success and close attention paid to coherence with other goals.

Source: Freeman and Soete, 1997, p. 415.

A major difficulty for environmental policy is how to promote sustainable technologies within a market economy that selects products and processes, not on the basis of environmental criteria but on the basis of profitability, which in turn is influenced by demand, often foreign demand. A way through this difficulty is to develop policies that can take advantage of the cumulative and self-reinforcing characteristics of technical change by guiding industry's continual search for innovations and technologies towards environmentally beneficial directions. Ideally, the process would be self-reinforcing in that additional searches for new technical solutions would follow within the same technical pathway. For example, experience gained from generating electricity from photovoltaic cells in the few situations where this technology is economically competitive should lead to learning effects that gradually improve the cost-effectiveness of photovoltaic cells and so increase their competitiveness. Increasing competitiveness should then attract additional investment in the technology, leading to further technical improvements and cost reductions and a higher number of economically feasible applications. These effects have already been demonstrated in the falling costs of wind power and other sources of renewable energy in many countries.

There are three main policy tools to guide private firms towards investing in the development of environmentally sustainable technologies: direct regulation, economic instruments and procurement. Each is briefly discussed in turn; each one raises fundamental challenges for global application.

Direct regulation, for example through air, water, soil and product quality standards, or through limitations on the conditions and use of a product, is probably the most common method for reducing pollution or exposure to hazardous substances. At an international level such regulations will, practically by definition, vary widely between countries/regions. To the extent that particular emissions have in the first instance a local impact, such variety is understandable – even though specific problems can arise in cross-border regions. In areas with a more significant global impact – climate change, ocean pollution, overfishing, etc. – achieving worldwide agreement on a regulatory framework will be difficult to achieve, as is obvious from the limited progress made in those areas. Regulations have also been extensively criticised, on theoretical grounds, as less efficient than economic instruments as a means of promoting innovation in less polluting technologies.

Economic instruments include tradable emission permits, emission and product taxes, and in some cases subsidies (although subsidies are also discussed below as part of procurement). Economic instruments differ from direct regulation in that they do not set standards for emissions. Pollution is permitted, but at a direct cost to the polluter ("the polluter must pay"). Economic instruments function through policies that estimate the externality costs of pollution and attach these costs to the inputs or outputs of production. For example, high-sulphur fuels could be taxed to include the estimated costs of environmental damage from acid rain. The additional cost to industry should attract innovative activity to find alternative fuels or new technologies that can reduce sulphur emissions. Since at the international level nothing would prevent the trading or exchange of such permits, it is obvious that there is a need for (international) regulatory control of these markets.

More generally, the efficient use of economic instruments is dependent on better accounting practices to estimate environmental costs, and on technologies to measure emissions accurately. Up to now these have proved to be major obstacles, particularly in an international environment in which such activities are often nationally organised. Nevertheless, resources could be raised to focus on international investment in developing real-time monitoring systems for a range of substances, controlled by independent international institutions. An additional but complementary need is to identify and remove perverse economic instruments, such as tax credits and subsidies in agriculture, that support environmentally harmful practices.

International (like national) procurement policies can, either through the direct support of research and development or through subsidising the use or development of environmentally beneficial technologies within private firms, play an important role in achieving the goal of environmentally sustainable development. Direct procurement is probably most appropriate for the development of new technologies for use in infrastructure systems, such as energy, transportation and waste disposal systems, allowing to some degree a process of technological "catching up" if not "leap-frogging". Subsidies or aid programmes, for example through tax credits or co-operative research projects between industry and public research institutes, may be the most effective means of developing cleaner process technologies where much of the existing knowledge is held by private firms and has not been codified or made publicly available.

The essential goal of such policies is to encourage the rapid international diffusion of environmentally beneficial technologies. Diffusion can, however, also be enhanced by programmes that increase the number of people that are knowledgeable about the innovation and capable of applying it to the needs of industry. Policies to support demonstration projects and technology transfer programmes can help by increasing exposure to a range of potential users. Procurement programmes based on incrementalist principles can also encourage the rapid diffusion of best-practice technologies by increasing the number of individuals with direct knowledge of the technology and the ability to use it within the private sector.

The goal of environmentally sustainable development entails the development and application of a wide range of technologies, each of which follows a unique pattern. The large number of technologies, needs and applications means that governments lack the necessary information to decide the details of the innovation needed to solve particular problems. Much can thus be gained from international exchange and collaboration. At the same time, instead of defining solutions, policies should be designed to influence the incentives that firms face, as discussed above, and to support research programmes that build upon the enormous diversity of the sources and applications of innovations by ensuring that the widest possible range of potentially beneficial technologies are explored and developed. This can be achieved through research and procurement programmes that involve innovating firms, the potential users of new products and processes, public research institutions, and non-governmental organisations. In addition, to make sure that a wide range of potential applications are also explored, these programmes to develop new technologies should also include many firms that could potentially benefit from them. This last point is particularly pertinent, given the importance of knowledge and the unique ways in which technologies are used by different firms.

Both radical "breakthrough" technologies and incremental improvements to existing technologies are needed. An example of a future breakthrough innovation is solar (or another renewable) energy technology, which could acquire a central role in an environmentally sustainable economy. An example of an incremental innovation with environmentally beneficial effects is a technical adapter for jet aircraft engines to increase fuel efficiency and reduce NOx emissions.

It should be noted that the term "incrementalism" is used by several researchers to describe a specific approach to the innovation process rather than to the taxonomic type of innovation. An incrementalist innovation process can produce both incremental and radical innovations. The basic principle is that the innovation process should be designed to encourage frequent evaluations of a developing technology by a large number of researchers or potential users. This can be achieved through the use of relatively short development times for each technical advance, small project sizes, low capital investment levels for each project, and a minimum need for a dedicated infrastructure with no other uses. The latter three criteria are designed to allow a range of firms and research institutions to conduct parallel research projects in a given technology in order to increase the opportunities for a large number of people both to evaluate the technology critically, either through the rigours of the market or through non-market means, and to use the results of these evaluations to guide further technical developments.

The goal of an incrementalist approach to the innovation process is to avoid over-investment in a limited range of expensive technologies that are later found to be unworkable, overly expensive or environmentally more harmful than the technologies they were designed to replace. This is a potential problem with mission-oriented projects to develop radical new technologies through large, expensive, long-term projects that limit the number of participants to a few technically advanced firms or research institutes. However, one or more incrementalist principles may need to be waived in cases where they would completely preclude the exploration of a potentially beneficial technology.

Organisations that can increase the external international pressure on firms include, in addition to government, research institutes, the environmental technology sector, and NGOs – non-governmental (*e.g.* consumer, public health, environmental) organisations. NGOs can increase pressure on firms by influencing demand through raising consumer awareness of environmental issues and of poor corporate practices. German consumer organisations appear to have been particularly effective in exerting this type of pressure.

Internal pressure can be placed on firms through trade and industry organisations and by the environmental and marketing departments within private firms. These organisations can alter acceptable practice by ensuring that environmental issues are included as an important factor in long-term strategy. There is also a need for more social science research, to increase our understanding of both the capabilities of organisations and individuals to adapt to environmental goals and the design of appropriate policies to encourage this process.

The goal of environmentally sustainable development requires a wide range of complementary policies to support investment in new environmental technologies and the rapid diffusion of successful applications. These policies – while often national in nature, supporting *e.g.* the competitiveness of industry and its capacity to change – do have their international counterpart.

Policies to develop environmental technologies can help to improve the competitiveness of industry in at least two ways. First, new technologies that reduce the amount of material and energy inputs per unit of output will, on average, also reduce costs. Second, policies that guide innovation towards the development of products and processes that meet stringent standards for environmental performance and safety can also increase the global competitiveness of industry if these standards are likely to be demanded in the future by many different countries. But international agreements on environmental regulations, as probably the most explicit expression of positive integration, do raise formidable policy challenges.

As *The Economist* put it, "environmental problems rarely respect national borders". The waste products created by industry or consumers in one country can be spread *via* air or water across many other countries or even globally, as with CFCs. Alternatively, the waste products produced by a large number of countries can be deposited in a single country or region. Given the international character of environmental problems, the goal of environmentally sustainable development is important to all of the different regions and nations of the world, and requires the widespread diffusion of new technologies and supporting institutions. The multinational character of both the problems and the solutions suggests a strong role for supra-national organisations such as the UN; at the same time the localised nature of many of the sources of pollution, and differences in the institutions and solutions that have developed to solve environmental problems (*e.g.* to dispose of or recycle household and industrial waste) require the extensive involvement of regional and national governments. For this reason, environmentally sustainable development can only be attained by the active involvement of all levels of government. This requires careful application of the subsidiarity principle in order to determine the responsibilities at each level. (The "subsidiarity principle" may be defined as leaving decision-making to the lowest possible level consistent with the efficient fulfilment of the responsibility in each case.)

Obviously in the case of a federal government, such as those of Germany, the United States or Canada, the division of responsibilities would depend on the specific constitutional, legal and political circumstances; nonetheless, the principle of subsidiarity is a useful guideline for maximising local grass roots participation and minimising centralised bureaucracy. However, consideration of the case of the European Union or of the federal government in the United States shows that there are many responsibilities that are best undertaken at higher levels, or jointly by supra-national, federal, national and local authorities. Hopefully in the next century, worldwide intercontinental agencies will be able to assume greater responsibility for global standards in order to help countries avoid the problem of loss of national or regional competitive advantage through strong environmental policies, *e.g.* carbon tax, etc.

Defining and developing consensus around specific environmental goals are, however, thorny problems, particularly when those goals require substantial changes to systemic and interlocked technologies. For example, agriculture is a production and consumption system that includes not only farmers and consumers, but government subsidy and income support programmes as well as the suppliers of equipment, pesticides and fertilizers. The solution to the environmental problems caused by agriculture could require not only minor changes, such as the development of less toxic pesticides, but a change in the entire structure of agricultural production. Similarly, the goal of reducing energy consumption could require systemic changes in the complex transport infrastructures that have developed over the last century, in order to increase the attractiveness and flexibility of public transport in comparison with the private car. These types of major changes to the techno-economic system cannot be achieved without political debate. How to achieve such political debate at the global level, with the many different interests and trade-offs, is an area in which the OECD as well as other international organisations could contribute in the next century.

CONCLUSION

This chapter has focused on the institutional challenges brought about by the trend towards globalisation, in particular with respect to the creation, diffusion and use of new technologies. There are two areas in particular where globalisation (limited here to the real economy)[8] appears to be questioning traditional national policy-making and bringing to the forefront an urgent need for international policy action.

First, following the further liberalisation of trade and capital flows over the last decade, firms have increasingly directed their strategies to the joint aim of reaping the scale advantages of 1) worldwide presence, associated increasingly with some of their intangible investments and capabilities (technology, advertising, logistics, management), and 2) more production- and distribution-oriented local presence in some of the highly diversified geographical regions of the world – hence the concept of "glocalisation". Such global strategies, pursued by what have been called multi-domestic or network firms, increasingly question the meaning of much nationally focused – or, for that matter, European-focused – technology and industrial policy. To some extent one is now witnessing a repeat at the regional level of some of the previous national "strategic" arguments in favour of technology and industrial policy.

While international organisations, such as GATT and later on WTO, were set up to deal with the international liberalisation of goods, services and investment flows, and have over the years seen their mandate enlarged (WTO, WIPO), the scope and need for international policy action has nevertheless increased much more rapidly, going beyond the traditional, relatively-easy-to-achieve liberalisation and deregulation aspects of world integration (so-called "negative" integration). The nature of and need for "positive" integration, aiming at the development of a harmonized global regulatory framework, remain much more open to debate. In areas such as competition, intellectual property rights (as comparison between US, European and Japanese patent protection, copyrights or author rights illustrates), industrial or technology policies, there are major differences between the scope and nature of national policies. Yet, as illustrated in Section 2, each of these areas is essential with respect to both the creation and diffusion of new technologies. Each appears often to be based on a historically grown tissue of rather diverse and nationally oriented institutions. To transform or adapt these institutions to the new global environment is particularly difficult. Yet, there is little doubt that with the increasing complexity, risks and uncertainty involved in the creation and development of new technologies, there are clear advantages to *international* interaction, networking, alliances and the co-ordination and collaboration of national support policies. Similarly, given the worldwide opportunities for sharing knowledge and the diffusion of new technologies with "worldwide" problem-solving potential, national policies appear one-sided and in need of a global counterpart.

Probably nowhere is this more true than with respect to the environmental problems our planet is currently facing. Out of the broad list of issues, the fourth section focused on sustainable development. Here too, it is clear that solutions to some of the most urgent environmental problems will have to be found in the more efficient use of new technologies. National science and technology policies need to be refocused in the first instance on global collaboration and on world-wide technology diffusion. It could be argued that the social rate of return of such activities to the world as a whole is higher than individual countries' social rate of return. Considering the potential waste of resources at the world level because of the duplication of effort, co-ordination of research activities beyond national prestige must be an absolute priority. Again, though, such voluntary collaboration appears less and less sufficient compared with the rapidly growing global nature of the environmental problems confronting our planet. There appears a clear need for a global, nationally independent, international institution carrying out many of the national environmental technology diffusion policies reviewed in Section 4: imposing particular regulations, providing incentives for the creation of international tradable emission rights, taking public procurement initiatives.

As the recent cuts in the funding of international organisations by individual Member countries illustrates, guaranteeing the independence of such global institutions will require a more direct funding, independent of individual countries' democratic control, but directly based on a worldwide citizen contribution. The ultimate test of policy readiness to tackle these global issues lies not just in the readiness to create or broaden the scope of responsibilities of new or existing international institutions, but in national governments' readiness to "outsource" part of their national powers – powers that may appear democratic from a national perspective but less so from a world citizen perspective. It is from the latter perspective that proposals such as a worldwide tax on various features of global-isation – *e.g.* the Tobin tax, an international transport tax or electronic transmis-sion tax (the "bit tax") – take on real significance. Marginal taxing of some of the welfare gains associated with globalisation does not represent any particular country's protectionist or competitive interest; rather, it represents the contribu-tion (out of the jurisdiction of national governments) of the worldwide citizen to the planet's global problem-solving capacity.

NOTES

1. Suffice it to say that practically every OECD country still has some sort of competitiveness council or advisory group.
2. That is one of the reasons why the OECD is currently carrying out its G-7 follow-up project on this particular issue.
3. An interesting set of ideas has been put forward in this context by Geelhoed, 1997.
4. For conflicting views, see among others Ohmae (1990), Patel and Pavitt (1991), Pearce and Singh (1992), Scherer (1992), Dunning (1993) and Archibugi and Michie (1995). For a recent overview of the literature, see Archibugi and Michie (1997).
5. See in particular the various contributions in Siebert, 1997.
6. For more details see Freeman and Soete, 1997.
7. One can interpret the measures of best-practice and average technical progress developed in Soete and Turner (1984) in this sense.
8. Given the focus of this contribution, the main aspects of financial globalisation are by and large ignored.

BIBLIOGRAPHY

ARCHIBUGI, D. and J. MICHIE (1995), "The Globalisation of Technology: A New Taxonomy", *Cambridge Journal of Economics*, 19, pp. 121-140.

ARCHIBUGI, D. and J. MICHIE, eds. (1997), *Technology, Globalisation and Economic Performance*, Cambridge University Press, Cambridge.

ARTHUR, W.B. (1995), *Increasing Returns and Path Dependence in the Economy*, The University of Michigan Press, Ann Arbor.

BIS (1996), *Annual Report*.

DAVID, P.A. and D. FORAY (1995), "Accessing and Expanding the Science and Technology Knowledge Base: STI Outlook", *STI Review*, Vol. 16, OECD, Paris.

DOSI, G. (1984), *Technical Change and Industrial Transformation*, Macmillan, London.

DOSI, G., K. PAVITT and L. SOETE (1990), *The Economics of Technical Change and International Trade*, Wheatsheaf, Brighton.

DUNNING, J. (1993), *The Globalization of Business: The Challenge of the 1990s*, Routledge, London.

EUROPEAN UNION (1997), *Building the European Information Society for Us All*, High-Level Expert Group, Final Report, EU, Brussels.

FORAY, D. and B.-A. LUNDVALL (1996), *Employment and Growth in the Knowledge-based Economy*, OECD, Paris.

FREEMAN, C. (1987), *Technology Policy and Economic Performance: Lessons from Japan*, Pinter, London.

FREEMAN, C. and L. SOETE (1994), *Work for All or Mass Unemployment: Computerised Technical Change into the 21st Century*, Pinter, London.

FREEMAN, C. and L. SOETE (1997), *The Economics of Industrial Innovation*, Third Edition, Creative Print and Design, London.

GEELHOED, L.A. (1997), "1997: Een delta in Europa", *ESB*, 1 January, pp. 4-8.

HOWITT, P. (1996), *The Implications of Knowledge-Based Growth for Micro-Economic Policies*, The University of Calgary Press, Calgary.

LUNDVALL, B.-A. (1992), *National Systems of Innovation: Towards a Theory of Innovation and Interactive Learning*, Pinter, London.

MANSFIELD, E. (1995), *Innovation, Technology and the Economy, Selected Essays*, 2 Vols., Elgar, Aldershot.

NARULA, R. (1996), "Forms of International Cooperation between Corporations" in C. Jepma and A. Rhoen (eds.), *International Trade: A Business Perspective*, Longman, Harlow, pp. 98-122.

NELSON, R. (1992), "What Has Been the Matter with Neoclassical Growth Theory?" in G. Silverberg and L. Soete (eds.), *The Economics of Growth and Technical Change*, Elgar, Aldershot.

OECD (1991), *Technology in a Changing World*, Paris.

OECD (1992), *Technology and the Economy: The Key Relationships*, Paris.

OECD (1993), *The OECD Response*, Interim Report by the Secretary-General, Paris.

OECD (1996), *The OECD Job Strategy: Technology, Productivity and Job Creation*, Vols. I and II, Paris.

OHMAE, K. (1990), *The Borderless World*, Harper, New York.

PATEL, P. and K. PAVITT (1991), "Large Firms in the Production of the World's Technology: An Important Case of 'Non-globalisation'", *Journal of International Business Studies*, Vol. 22, pp. 1-21.

PAVITT, K. (1984), "Patterns of Technical Change: Towards a Taxonomy and a Theory", *Research Policy*, Vol. 13, No. 6, pp. 343-73.

PAVITT, K. and P. PATEL (1998), "Global Corporations and National Systems of Innovation: Who Dominates Whom?" in J. Howells and J. Mitchie (eds.), *National Systems of Innovation or the Globalisation of Technology*, Cambridge University Press, Cambridge.

PEARCE, R. and S. SINGH (1992), *Globalizing Research and Development*, Macmillan, London.

SCHERER, F.M. (1992), *International High-Technology Competition*, Harvard University Press, Cambridge, Mass.

SIEBERT, H., ed. (1997), *Towards a New Global Framework for High-Technology Competition*, J.C.B. Mohr, Tübingen.

SOETE, L. (1997), "The Impact of Globalization on European Economic Integration", *The ITPS Report*, No. 15, pp. 21-28.

SOETE, L. and R. TURNER. (1984), "Technology Diffusion and the Rate of Technical Change", *Economic Growth and the Structure of Long-Term Development*, St. Martin's Press, New York.

TIDD, J. et al. (1997), *Managing Innovation: Integrating Technological, Market and Organizational Change*, Wiley, Chichester.

LIST OF PARTICIPANTS

CHAIRMAN

Donald JOHNSTON
Secretary-General
OECD

PARTICIPANTS

Werner ARBER
Nobel Laureat
Professor of Genetics
Biozentrum
University of Basel
Switzerland

Walter S. BAER
Vice President
RAND Corporation
United States

Simon BEST
CEO and Managing Director
Zeneca Plant Science
United Kingdom

Walter BRINKMANN
Senior Vice President
Coca Cola Europe
Belgium

Roberto CARNEIRO
President
Grupo Forum
former Minister of Education
Portugal

Joseph F. COATES
President
Coates & Jarratt, Inc.
United States

P.S. DEODHAR
Chairman
Mahanager Gas Ltd
former Chairman of the Electronics
Commission of the Indian Government
India

Frederik A. von DEWALL
General Manager and Chief Economist
ING Bank
The Netherlands

Meinolf DIERKES
Professor and Director
Abteilung Organisation und
Technikgenese
Wissenschaftszentrum Berlin
Germany

Emilio FONTELA
Professor of Economics
University of Madrid
Spain

Hervé GALLAIRE
Vice President
Xerox Research Centre Europe
France

Orhan GÜVENEN
Undersecretary
State Planning Organisation
Prime Minister's Office
Turkey

Ian HARVEY
Chief Executive
BTG plc.
United Kingdom

Makoto KURODA
Secretary-General
Japanese Association
for the 2005 World Exposition
former Vice-Minister,
Ministry of International Trade
and Industry (MITI)
Japan

Reinhold LEITTERSTORF
Director General
Federal Ministry of Education,
Science, Research and Technology
Germany

Wolfgang LIEB
Secretary of State
Ministry for Science and Research
Northrhine-Westfalia
Germany

Ulf MERBOLD
Scientific Astronaut
European Astronaut Centre
European Space Agency (ESA)
Germany

Wolfgang MICHALSKI
Director,
Advisory Unit to the Secretary-General
OECD

Paolo MONFERINO
Executive Vice President
FIAT Spa
Italy

Hans Henning OFFEN
Vice Chairman of the Managing Board
Westdeutsche Landesbank
Germany

Erik ØVERLAND
Advisor
Ministry of National Planning
and Coordination
Norway

Werner POLLMANN
Senior Vice President
Daimler-Benz AG
Germany

Grégoire POSTEL-VINAY
Chef de l'Observatoire des Stratégies
Industrielles
Ministère de l'Économie, des Finances
et de l'Industrie
France

Bernard ROCQUEMONT
Président Directeur Général
Thomson CSF
France

Jorma ROUTTI
Director-General
DG XII: Science, Research
and Development
European Commission

Hanspeter SCHELLING
Chairman, Research Advisory Board
Novartis International AG
Switzerland

Walter SCHUSSER
Vice President
Siemens AG
Germany

Ms Tayce A. WAKEFIELD
Member of the Board of Directors
General Motors of Canada Ltd.
Canada

Luc SOETE
Director
Maastricht Economic Research Institute
for Innovation and Technology
The Netherlands

Huijiong WANG
Vice President, Academic Committee
Development Research Center
The State Council
China

OECD SECRETARIAT

Barrie STEVENS
Deputy Head, Advisory Unit
to the Secretary-General

Riel MILLER
Principal Administrator, Advisory Unit
to the Secretary-General

Pierre-Alain SCHIEB
Principal Administrator, Advisory Unit
to the Secretary-General

OECD PUBLICATIONS, 2, rue André-Pascal, 75775 PARIS CEDEX 16
PRINTED IN FRANCE
(03 98 03 1 P) ISBN 92-64-16052-3 – No. 50119 1998